ISBN 978-0-260-88293-6
PIBN 11192759

1 MONTH OF
FREE
READING

at

www.ForgottenBooks.com

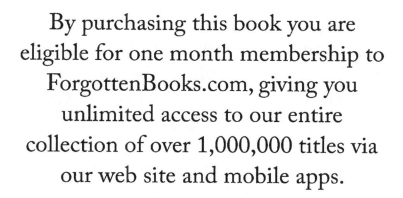

By purchasing this book you are eligible for one month membership to ForgottenBooks.com, giving you unlimited access to our entire collection of over 1,000,000 titles via our web site and mobile apps.

To claim your free month visit:
www.forgottenbooks.com/free1192759

English
Français
Deutsche
Italiano
Español
Português

www.forgottenbooks.com

Mythology Photography **Fiction**
Fishing Christianity **Art** Cooking
Essays Buddhism Freemasonry
Medicine **Biology** Music **Ancient**
Egypt Evolution Carpentry Physics
Dance Geology **Mathematics** Fitness
Shakespeare **Folklore** Yoga Marketing
Confidence Immortality Biographies
Poetry **Psychology** Witchcraft
Electronics Chemistry History **Law**
Accounting **Philosophy** Anthropology
Alchemy Drama Quantum Mechanics
Atheism Sexual Health **Ancient History**
Entrepreneurship Languages Sport
Paleontology Needlework Islam
Metaphysics Investment Archaeology
Parenting Statistics Criminology
Motivational

PENNSYLVANIA COMMISSION

on

OLD AGE ASSISTANCE

———————

JANUARY, 1925

LETTER OF TRANSMITTAL

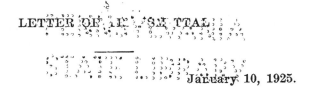

January 10, 1925.

TO THE GENERAL ASSEMBLY OF THE COMMONWEALTH OF PENNSYLVANIA:

Because of the interest manifested in the subject of old age assistance we are not satisfied to present in this report only the findings of our last year's researches. In order to give an up-to-date, coordinated and logical story of the entire subject, we deemed it essential to submit, in addition, a brief statement of the facts and disclosures previously recorded regarding the conditions of the aged in Pennsylvania as well as a summary of the conclusions reached by the various Commissions which have studied the bewildering system of our poor laws. These reveal that we are now operating under a system of poor relief based on principles inaugurated in the Elizabethan Poor Law of 1601. AT THE PRESENT TIME, THERE ARE FIVE HUNDRED AND EIGHTY-THREE SEPARATE POOR DISTRICTS UNDER EIGHT DIFFERENT SYSTEMS OF ADMINISTRATION.

Our studies of the aged men and women who have applied for assistance under the Old Age Assistance Act bear out fully the crying need for effective old age provision in the Commonwealth of Pennsylvania:

(1) Although 90 PER CENT OF THE APPLICANTS ARE NATIVE BORN, THE AVERAGE TOTAL POSSESSIONS OF THE APPLICANTS EXAMINED IS LESS THAN $24 PER PERSON WHILE THE AVERAGE AMOUNT OF SAVINGS IS ONLY $6.75 PER APPLICANT.

(2) THREE OUT OF EVERY FOUR APPLICANTS ARE WITHOUT ANY REMUNERATIVE OCCUPATION AND DEPENDENT FOR SUPPORT.

(3) While the children of the applicants, in however humble conditions, were generally found to make every effort to support their parents, these children were in many instances in no position to do so because of the inadequacy of their own income and the size of their families. Not infrequently these parents were supported at the expense of their own children's welfare.

(4) Many aged men and women who have no children to help them are already supported either by their respective poor districts, private charity organizations, or private individuals—in other words, with moneys coming from the taxpayers.

L304500

4

(5) That many of the aged, with but slight assistance from the State, could find adequate homes have been fully brought out by our investigations.

(6). A perusal of our findings will prove conclusively that in the great majority of instances THE FAILURE TO ADEQUATELY PROTECT THEMSELVES IN OLD AGE WAS NOT DUE TO INDIVIDUAL MALADJUSTMENT OR "BLAME," but were a result of conditions and circumstances over which these unfortunate aged had no control. This is fully supported by the statements of facts, the testimonials of the county boards and the former employers of the applicants.

(7) Neither the almshouse nor the present system of our outdoor poor relief adequately meet the needs of these worthy aged. They are costly both financially and spiritually. AN EFFECTIVE STATE ASSISTANCE SYSTEM APPEALS TO US AS THE ONLY ADEQUATE ALTERNATIVE UNDER PRESENT CONDITIONS.

(8) Old Age Pension systems abroad are meeting with the hearty approval of their people and are spreading everywhere.

(9) That the overwhelming majority of public opinion in Pennsylvania is insistent upon a fitting old age assistance plan is fully borne out by the editorial comments, letters from employers and the proceedings of the Old Age Assistance Conference held on November 13th, summaries of which are given in the report.

The opponents of this law have broadcast information throughout the State that the present law would cost the State at least $25,000,000 a year. Inasmuch as they do not at all present any figures supporting this ridiculous sum, we unhesitatingly and categorically declare these figures to be without foundation or reason.

Based upon as accurate and scientific figures as are ascertainable, we find that even if every aged person in the State, qualified under the law, would be given assistance, THE COST WOULD NOT AMOUNT TO MORE THAN, APPROXIMATELY, $5,000,000. A YEAR, OR ABOUT 57 CENTS FOR EACH CITIZEN IN THE STATE. This is a big sum of money until it is re-called that FOR THIS SUM WE WOULD BE ABLE TO TAKE CARE OF THREE TIMES THE NUMBER OF PERSONS NOW TAKEN CARE OF IN OUR ALMSHOUSES WHICH EXPENDITURES, IF EVERYTHING BE INCLUDED, AMOUNT TO AT LEAST $8,000,000 A YEAR. We firmly believe that there is not a citizen in this Commonwealth who would not rather be willing to pay his 57 cents, WHICH IS BUT 56 CENTS PER $1,000 TAXABLE PROPERTY AND ONLY 24 CENTS PER $1,000 WEALTH OF THE STATE—even of these were additional, which happily is not the case—than be responsible for the tragedies and heart-breaks now caused by the prospect of the poorhouse after a lifetime of toil and service.

Furthermore, OF THE APPROXIMATELY $6,200,000 CASH SPENT ON OUR ALMSHOUSES IN THE YEAR 1922, AT LEAST $3,000,000 OF THE TOTAL WAS SPENT ON THE ADMINISTRATION OF THE SYSTEM; ONLY ABOUT HALF GOING DIRECTLY TO THE INMATES. IT TOOK OVER 1,000 PAID EMPLOYEES TO LOOK AFTER THE 8,000 INMATES OF OUR ALMSHOUSES. THESE INSTITUTIONS ALSO REPORT A VALUE OF LAND, BUILDING AND EQUIPMENT OF OVER $16,000,000, AND OWN OVER 17,000 ACRES OF LAND OF WHICH MORE THAN 10,000 WERE REPORTED TO BE UNDER CULTIVATION.

Even under liberal estimates, we are convinced, from studies of the facts, that UNDER THE PRESENT LAW A FUND OF $5,000,000 A YEAR WOULD NOT REQUIRE FOR ADMINISTRATIVE EXPENSES—FOR BOTH STATE AND COUNTIES— A SUM TO EXCEED $300,000 PER YEAR, WHICH IS BUT SIX PER CENT OF THE TOTAL AS AGAINST ALMOST FIFTY PER CENT UNDER THE COUNTY ALMSHOUSE SYSTEM. The cost for investigation per applicant in the 26 counties from which figures were obtained shows that THE AVERAGE COST PER APPLICANT AMOUNTS TO $1.04, OR LESS THAN 41 CENTS PER $100 allowed.

We are deeply aggrieved that we were unable to come to the assistance of at least some of our worthy aged. Perhaps the earthly lives of some of those already gone to their eternal rest could have been somewhat prolonged even with the meagre appropriations allowed us by the last Legislature. We know that by placing the Old Age Assistance Act on the statute books, the sunset days of the aged were made brighter with renewed hope for the future. The court proceedings against the constitutionality of the Act, however, blocked our plans and shattered our hopes in that direction. No doubt by the time this is read the State Supreme Court will have rendered its decision on the question of the constitutionality of the Old Age Assistance Act. We trust the law will be sustained.* But, regardless of the legal or technical points involved, we are convinced that, as representatives of the great Commonwealth of Pennsylvania, you are fully conscious of the enormous need of this beneficient law. The findings in this report have proven this. We respectfully recommend the reading of the entire report for a more thorough understanding of the problem. We are confident that once the facts are familiar, the thousands of our loyal, aged citizens whose hopes have been so much encouraged will not be forsaken and immediate assistance will be provided for them. This is our cherished hope and prayer.

---

*On Feb. 2, 1925, the Supreme Court rendered a decision declaring the Old Age Assistance Act unconstitutional.

Whatever success we have achieved in securing this wealth of information and in bringing forth this Report is, of course, not exclusively the result of our efforts. We wish to record our debt to the General Assembly of 1923 and Governor Gifford Pinchot for making possible the procuring of this information; to the public press in the State we are indebted for the liberal editorial and news space which they generously accorded our work; last, but not least, we must acknowledge our deepest gratitude to the members of the various county boards, who have given so generously and so much of their unselfish labor and whose devotion to this just cause was largely responsible for the obtaining of these data. The day when an adequate Old Age Assistance law is inaugurated in Pennsylvania will be, we know, a most happy one to all these as well as to ourselves.

Respectfully submitted:

JAMES H. MAURER,
Chairman
MARY V. GRICE,
DAVID S. LUDLUM.

ANDREW P. BOWER,
Superintendent.
ABRAHAM EPSTEIN,
Executive Secretary.

CONTENTS

CHAPTER I.

's interest in behalf of the aged and dependent poor
.ame and establishment as a Commonwealth of the
Even prior to the granting of Penn's Charter in
)ut in operation by the Duke of York, in the territory
nsylvania, provided for contributions from each town
for the purposes of the poor. The Great Law passed
held at Chester in 1682, stipulated that the Justices
ιall make provision for the poor in such way as they
aient.

Early Pennsylvania Legislation

de of the English poor laws adapted to Pennsylvania
n 1771, and the first almshouse established in the
was that of Philadelphia in 1773. The Act of 1771
made perpetual by an Act passed April 6, 1776. But
having been passed by the provincial government, it
ecessary to pass the Act of March 4, 1778. Later,
statutes were superseded by a law passed March 25,
vived, re-enacted and perpetuated the foregoing law,
771, which was based upon the English poor laws,
e the law of the State until the passing of the general
336, which in turn, was substantially a re-enactment
w, as no change of any consequence was made in the
y significant change in the law of 1879 was the pro-
tdoor relief may be granted in exceptional cases but
all be entitled to claim such relief who refuses to go
)rhouse."

ι Poor Law Basis for Present Pennsylvania Law

problem of what to do and how best to provide for
he dependent in the community has been faced since
nial days; it has been met in various ways and in
:th the enlightened policies of the period. However,
the first two centuries of the white man's rule of this
)visions for relief of the dependent poor were con-

have, during the same period, witnessed practically no basic change in our general policy of public poor relief, especially that concerning the dependent aged. Although, in England, the poor law upon which our system is modeled, has been greatly modified, in the case of the children, by the Reform Bill of 1833; and, in the case of the aged, the almshouse was completely substituted wherever possible by the Old Age Pension Act of 1908, we, in Pennsylvania today, are confronted with a system of poor relief that really dates back to the original Elizabethan Poor Law of 1601. A study of the English poor law system convinces that the laws in force in Pennsylvania today are identical in principle and almost identical in language with the famous poor laws of Queen Elizabeth.

Consequent Confusion

As a result, instead of a simple unified system of poor relief which would deal adequately with the various dependent classes, we have in Pennsylvania a bewildering system of local and general legislation embodied in nearly 3,000 Acts of Assembly which deal variously with local, county and state phases of the problem. This was inevitable, inasmuch, as the needs grew, remedial measures had to be adopted regardless of the fundamental law. The tendency in our poor relief administration having been away from uniformity, each locality sought to relieve and remedy its own conditions through such legislation as it deemed best for its own welfare. Consequently, we now frequently find the same parts or units of the State under local laws which show considerable differences. Thus, it is interesting to note in what variegated fashion our poor laws are administered throughout the State today. IN TWENTY-EIGHT COUNTIES, POOR RELIEF IS ADMINISTERED BY A SEPARATE BOARD OF DIRECTORS OF THE POOR; IN SIXTEEN COUNTIES, THE COUNTY COMMISSIONERS ALSO ACT AS DIRECTORS OF THE POOR; IN SEVENTEEN OTHER COUNTIES, POOR RELIEF IS ADMINISTERED ON THE TOWNSHIP UNIT SYSTEM BY DIRECTORS OF THE POOR OR OVERSEERS IN EVERY TOWNSHIP, WHILE IN SIX OTHER COUNTIES, A MIXED SYSTEM COMBINING FEATURES OF ALL THE ABOVE, PREVAILS.

We have the Middle Coal Field Poor District, which is made up of Carbon County and a part of Luzerne County; the Central Poor District composed of another portion of Luzerne County, including Wilkes-Barre, while Jenkins Township, Pittston City and Pittstown Township Poor District include portions of Luzerne and Lackawanna Counties. In McKean County, the County Commissioners have jurisdiction over the poor in the entire county except in the city of Bradford, which is administered by a separate Board; while in

Allegheny, the Department of Charities has jurisdiction over the city, and the County Directors of the Poor supervise the rest of the County—each maintaining separate almshouses.

Even more confusing and bewildering is the situation in Philadelphia, where the Department of Public Welfare has charge of the City Poor Relief, while, at the same time—inside the walls of the city—the township of Bristol, occupying the greater part of the forty-second ward is managed by a Board of Guardians of the township of Bristol; the township of Germantown—comprising the twenty-second ward—is managed by a Board of Managers of the Poor of the Township of Germantown; a separate Board of Directors of the Poor exists also for the Roxboro Poor District, comprising parts of the twenty-second, twenty-third, thirty-fifth, forty-first and forty-second wards; while the township of Oxford and lower Dublin comprising parts of the twenty-third, thirty-fifth and forty-first wards, has a separate Board of Directors of the Poor. Byberry, comprising a part of the thirty-fifth ward, and Moreland Township, a part of the thirty-fifth ward, are under separate poor districts. In addition to the large Philadelphia almshouse, separate poorhouses are maintained by the respective poor districts in Germantown, Oxford and Lower Dublin and Roxboro. How bewildering all this is, is apparent from the fact that the forty-first and twenty-third wards are managed by two separate boards of poor directors, while the thirty-fifth ward is under the jurisdiction of four different kinds of poor boards.

CHAPTER II.

CRITICISMS OF PENNSYLVANIA POOR LAWS

The Commission of 1833

Our lethargy and neglect of this fundamental legislation seems even more surprising when it is reflected that warnings against this endless and jumbling tendency of local legislation of poor laws have been sounded in this State again and again for nearly a century. Indeed, this system has been attacked by every commission that was delegated to study the problem. As early as 1833, a Commission appointed to revise the laws of the State urged that "townships should be assimilated to counties, in respect to the mode of government, for the sake of regularity in the system," and, while, they contended, they did not "consider themselves at liberty" to dispense with the separate office of the Overseer of the Poor, they declared themselves as "not satisfied that any necessity exists for its continuance." The Commission further declared: "that there are defects in the system, and abuse in its practice, seems to be agreed upon all hands."

The Commission of 1889

In 1889, a Commission appointed by Governor James A Beaver indicted this extravagant policy in the following words:

"Up to the time of the adoption of the present state constitution, 1873, seventy-eight special poor-law districts were created by the legislature, and about three hundred and twenty-one acts of assembly passed relating to them. These districts were variously composed of counties, cities, boroughs, townships and unions or combinations of several different divisions. Of the seventy-eight special districts thus created, seventy-one are now maintaining almshouses or poorhouses; thirty-seven of which are county institutions and thirty-four belong to minor sub-divisions. Some of these districts have Directors of the Poor, some have Overseers. In some the taxes are levied and collected through the County Commissioners; in others, through borough and city authorities and in others through the township officials. In some, justices of the peace have the power to order relief to be given; in others, relief is given alone upon the order of the Directors of the Poor. In some, relief outside of the poorhouse or other institutions is given extensively, while in others, it is curtailed and allowed only under exceptional circumstances. In some of the districts, the directors and overseers are elected by the people, in others the directors are appointed by the court of quarter sessions of the county. In Philadelphia, there are neither directors nor overseers, but a Board of Charities and Corrections appointed by the Mayor, and responsible to him. In some districts, the directors or overseers are paid a daily or yearly sum ranging from a few dollars to several hundreds of dollars; and these sums are variously fixed, in some cases by an act of the Legislature, in others by the court, while in others, the auditors have the power to allow what they deem just. In Philadelphia, the president and directors of the Department of Charities receive no compensation, while in Pittsburgh the chief of the Department of Charities receives a salary of four thousand dollars per annum. These differences as to the areas of the districts, taxation, selection of officials, their number and powers, their compensation, etc., seem to be irreconcilable." ...

"In addition to the special laws which we have referred to above, there should also be mentioned the fact that about four hundred and fifty-six boroughs were erected under special charters and that over thirty-five hun-

dred acts were passed relative to them. When it is
known that most of these boroughs were authorized to
elect overseers of the poor, the utter impossibility of
reconciling this legislation by any codification must be
apparent."

The Commission went on to state:

"The statute books from the foundation of the government are strewn with special acts. The late Chief
Justice Woodward remarked in a case before the Supreme Court, that it was difficult, if not impossible, for
any lawyer to state the condition of the law relative
to local matters in any district with accuracy. When
the fact is mentioned that there are in the neighbor-
hood of eight hundred acts of assembly upon the statute books which relate, directly or indirectly, to the
poor laws, this difficulty will become apparent." This
number, it is now estimated, is more nearly 3,000 than
800·

Defects of the Law as found by Commission of 1889

Analyzing each phase of the inadequacy of the present poor relief system, the Commission in a scholarly report pointed out that:

"1. Relief is given commonly to the able-bodied without labor and the funds are used in other ways not con-
templated by the legislature and at the discretion of the
Directors and Overseers (of the Poor). In general too,
the payment of money for relief must be founded upon
the entry of the names of the person receiving relief
upon the poor book; but in many districts of the State
no poor book is kept and the business of the district is
conducted without any book.

"2. There is no general system of accounts in the
state....In the greater part of the state, the accounts
are kept and audited without any respect to the true
principles of the law, and as far as we know the taxpayers pay little attention to the subject.

"3. There is no uniformity in the administrative
areas....There are county districts, city districts, borough districts and union districts composed of parts of
counties or of several townships, boroughs, cities, etc.

"4. The laws of settlement are all derived through
the colonial and state legislation from the English Poor
Law.....No law has ever been passed in this state establishing irremovability in connection with the law relating to the removal of the poor, although this principle has been engrafted upon the laws of New Jersey
and perhaps one or two other of the states of the Union.

"5. Poor persons may still be removed in this commonwealth, whether chargeable or not, the original
provision as to the removability of persons likely to be-

come chargeable having been continued, although repealed in England at about the time of the revolution.... We believe that the costs and expenses of such removals are entirely out of proportion to any possible benefits that might accrue from such a practice....

"In one case, an overseer testified that he had caused the removal of a person likely to become chargeable, and it was said that the costs of such removal had amounted to one hundred and fifty dollars, and that the person had not in fact become chargeable.

"Another overseer said that 'people in his district are careful to see that paupers do not come into their district. Keep paupers out, is the rule. People who have houses to rent will not rent to a person likely to become chargeable. They freeze him out of the district'.

"Another one said: 'We go to men who own buildings and ask them not to rent to people liable to become a charge.'

"Another one: 'We do all we can to prevent people likely to become chargeable from gaining settlement, that is what overseers are for'

"A witness who had many years experience as an overseer made the following statement 'The principle duty of overseers now is to keep out paupers or those likely to become chargeable. They seem to elect hardhearted men for overseers, who, when a man applies for relief, abuse him so for becoming a pauper that he is entirely discourged and heart-broken. A great deal of money is spent in litigation that should be spent in relieving the poor. Under the present system, the children of paupers almost always become paupers. There have been cases of preventing a man registering and gaining residence. Some men are removed whom the overseers think will become chargeable.' "* .

* That things have not changed much since 1889 is obvious from the following reports of a field representative of the State Department of Welfare to his chief about the practice in one local poor district:

.February 28, 1923.
"On February 27, 1923, I investigated the complaint contained in attached letter. After interviewing the writer, the dependent, the wife of the Overseer of the Poor, the borough health officer and a few other people, I learned the following:
"Mr. C. leased a small brick two-room house to the Overseers of the Poor of the Borough at a rental of $8.00 per month, for the purpose of providing a home for Miss B, aged 78 years, a native of the town, who is dependent upon the charities of the community.
About one year ago the Overseers purchased a ramshackle frame building for $800. It is situated about 20 feet from the track of the P. R. R. and is in a dilapidated, insanitary condition, without heating or lighting equipment, leaky roof and damp floors. I CONSIDER THE BUILDING WHOLLY UNFIT FOR USES INTENDED: The Overseers notified Mr. C. that after April 1st they will no longer pay rent for the present house occupied by Miss B. She has been told that a refusal to move into this building will result in the withdrawal of all relief. The Overseers have provided about three quarters of a ton of coal since last September and permit Miss B. to purchase food at the grocery. Mr. A, the grocer, stated that her store bills do not amount to $1.50 per week and that he has not rendered a bill to the Overseers since last September.
"My conclusions are these—that the threat of forced removal of Miss B to the insanitary building, IS DONE FOR THE PURPOSE OF RELIEVING THEM OF THEIR OBLIGATION. IT WAS STATED TO ME THAT ANYONE APPLYING FOR RELIEF IS GIVEN THE PREFERENCE TO LIVE IN THIS BUILDING, WHICH IS GENERALLY DECLINED, THEREBY RELIEVING THE OVERSEERS OF DUTY TO THE NEEDY.
"There is to be no matron or caretaker, no lights other than oil lamps, no provision for comfort or care, only the offer of this building, which is little better than a stable.
"Miss B. is becoming blind. Her present home is comfortable. Mrs. C. and neighbors give her food and the cost for maintaining her will not exceed $150 per year. Electric lights furnished by Mr. C. without additional cost. Miss B has five relatives in the town and vicinity. These people should be appealed to for aid. Mr. C. will, I believe, accept less rent for the present house now occupied by Miss B, providing the Overseers will agree to compromise this matter. NO AGED HUMAN BEING SHOULD BE PERMITTED TO OCCUPY THE HOUSE OWNED BY THE BOROUGH. THE METHOD PURSUED BY THE OVERSEERS TO RID THEMSELVES OF A HUMANE RESPONSIBILITY IS CONTEMPTIBLE."

"6. Very little effort has been made to utilize the labor of such of the poor receiving relief as are able to work.

"7. General out-door relief is commonly given throughout the state, with the exception of the city of Philadelphia, where it is confined to medicine and medical attendance. Such relief is not uncommonly given to able-bodied persons. In some counties and districts, the practice prevails of fixing the amount to be given to the applicants by the week or month without any limit as to time.** Again, outdoor relief is given in some districts in money, in others it is in money and in kind, while in others it is given in kind only.

"8. There has been no change made in the law, relating to the liability of persons to support the poor relatives since the introduction of the English law into Pennsylvania, but we have reason to believe that the law has been indifferently enforced." . . . All students of the problem are unanimous that this indictment made by the Commission in 1889, in its major aspects, still holds true today."

The State Dependents Commission, 1915.

None of these difficulties having been remedied, the State Dependents Commission, twenty-five years later, in its report of 1915, continued this assault upon our system of poor laws by asking for its correction through the repeal and amendment of existing statutes, and by the constructive enactment of new and comprehensive legislation. It concluded:

"The Commission believes that certain important changes should be effected in the nature and administration of the law as well as with those of the institutions of the Commonwealth which deal with the great question of dependency in all its phases...The Commission

---

July 13, 1923.

"On the above date I visited and further investigated the case of Miss B. From several sources I learned, that about March 31, 1923, the two Overseers of the poor, accompanied by the town constable and an employed attorney proceeded to the small house occupied by the aged woman and demanded admittance for purposes of evicting her. SHE REFUSED TO PERMIT THE OVERSEERS TO ENTER. THEY THEN REMOVED THE WINDOWS; OVERSEER L. LEAPED THROUGH THE WINDOW, GRASPED THIS DESPERATE 72-YEAR OLD LADY, HELD HER SEVERELY UNTIL PART OF THE POSSE COULD ALSO CLIMB THROUGH THE WINDOW TO UNLOCK THE DOOR, WHENCE HER FEW GOODS AND CHATTELS WERE REMOVED TO THE DILAPIDATED, UNSANITARY AND WHOLLY UNFIT PLACE PROVIDED FOR HER. She refused to accept of their official hospitality. A kindly neighbor hauled her belongings back to the home from which she was evicted, where she now is, slowly dying of dropsy. Medical attention is given her gratis by a local woman physician. Her rent, $7.00 per month, is being paid by contributors, food is donated by neighbors, meanwhile the dignity of official authority of Overseers has been vindicated.

"The Overseers succeeded in forcing this old lady to relinquish her claim for borough aid, through their brave and tactful action. AS WAS ORIGINALLY INTENDED, THE OVERSEERS HAVE RELIEVED THEMSELVES OF A RESPONSIBILITY BY ENDEAVORING TO PROVIDE A PLACE OF ABODE FOR AN AGED CREATURE OF MISFORTUNE, UNFITTED AS AN ABIDING PLACE FOR BEASTS.

"The doctor informed me that the object of eviction will not long continue to be a burden upon her friends or an annoyance to the Overseers of the Poor.

"As was stated to me, there were no casualties other than an aggravation of the gradual natural decline of Miss B., spinster."

**A very recent examination of poor relief methods disclosed a number of cases throughout the State where a number of women who have been placed on the records for poor relief many years ago because they were widowed mothers with dependent children, were still in receipt of same, although some of them have since married and their children have all grown up, married and are able to take care of themselves.

cannot too strongly urge upon the General Assembly its conviction that the time has come when the whole question of charitable and correctional administration within the Commonwealth must be put upon the soundest basis."

Regarding the status of our poor laws and the county almhouses, the State Dependents Commission repeated the facts that:

"1. There are one hundred poor districts and eighty almhouses in the sixty-seven (67) counties of Pennsylvania.

"2. There is no systematic arrangement of poor districts. In some instances the district is either—

    (a) A county,
    (b) Parts of two counties,
    (c) A city,
    (d) A borough,
    (e) A township,
    (f) Groups of townships,
    (g) A borough and a township.

"3. Many almhouses are located in remote and inaccessible parts of existing Poor Districts.

"4. Many existing almhouses are old, poorly planned, without adequate equipment and are indifferently managed.

"5. There is no uniformity in the laws relating to the appointment or election of poor directors who may serve as such; the proper and uniform title of such officials; types of approved plans for almhouses; management and accounting; taxation for support; inspection; segregation of sexes and classes of inmates; admissions and discharges; payments for support.

"6. The inmates are a very heterogeneous collection. They comprise insane, feeble-minded persons and epileptics; blind and deaf mutes; sufferers from chronic diseases; persons with criminal records; prostitutes; mothers of illegitimate children; orphaned and deserted children.

"7. There are 1,100 Acts of Assembly relating to the Poor, of which 800 are local and special laws. No general revision of these has taken place since 1836, and the result is a chaotic conglomeration of legal confusion."

The State Dependents Commission specifically recommended to:

"1. Repeal all the present statutes on the subject and enact one comprehensive law to govern poor relief.

"2. Re-arrange the Poor Districts, making the County the minimum unit, so as to promote a more economical, efficient and humane administration than at present exists.

"3. Make a thorough and careful classification of inmates so that none but the actually indigent aged and infirm shall be admitted and kept in these institutions."

The Commissioner of Public Welfare in his First Biennial Report in 1922 continued this indictment and declared:

> "The county homes have been so over-crowded and such an expense to the counties that for lack of proper funds for their support they have degenerated, in many instances, into a disgraceful condition in the smaller communities . . . . The general mingling of the various groups of dependents in these homes at the present time makes the proper care of any single group almost impossible, and pitiable is the condition of all."

CHAPTER III.

HISTORY OF OLD AGE PENSION MOVEMENT IN PENNSYLVANIA

Creation of Old Age Pension Commission 1917

Undoubtedly, the flagrant conditions, recited above, prompted former Governor William C. Sproul, when still a member of the State Senate, to introduce in the 1917 Legislature joint resolution No. 413, which in part read as follows:

> "Whereas, progressive legislation has been enacted in some States and nations, establishing a system of pensions for aged and incapacitated citizens, and a number of plans for accomplishing this result have been suggested at various times in Pennsylvania;
>
> "Therefore, be it resolved, That the Governor of this Commonwealth be, and he is hereby, authorized and directed to appoint a commission, to consist of seven reputable citizens of Pennsylvania, who shall serve without compensation other than for their reasonable expenses, to look into the general subject of old age pensions, and to investigate the various systems provided for this purpose in other nations and States, together with all the facts relating thereto, especially as bearing upon the industrial and other conditions prevailing in Pennsylvania, and with a view to their practical adaptability here."

Findings of Old Age Pension Commission

In accordance with the provisions of the resolution, the Old Age Pension Commission appointed by Governor Martin G. Brumbaugh submitted to your Honorable body in 1919 a most comprehensive report of its studies on the subject. In this report, the Commission presented the facts in regard to nativity, family connections, physical conditions, cause of disability, occupation engaged in, wages earned, sources of income, means of outside support, etc., gathered from interviewing 3,405 inmates, 50 years of age and over, in 60 almshouses in the State. The report also contained full statistics and like information in regard to 2,170 inmates of 65 fraternal and benevolent homes for the aged in the State. Considerable information was included concerning nearly 500 aged recipients of private relief agencies. Interesting facts were also presented with reference to aged persons, 50 years of age and over, in the State in general. The latter were ascertained from personal interviews held with nearly 4,500 aged men and women in Philadelphia, Pittsburgh and Reading.

Chief Causes of Old Age Dependency

The following are brief summaries of the findings of the Old Age Pension Commission:

In regard to family connections, it was found that while of those in the almshouses 40 per cent were single, 17 per cent married and 39 per cent widowed, the proportions among the aged who reside in their homes were five and one-half per cent single, 55 per cent married and 33 per cent widowed. It was also disclosed that while among the aged paupers sixty-three and one-half per cent had no children living, only 10.6 per cent of the old folks living at home had no children living.

Again, of the 3,405 aged almhouse inmates, only 436, or less than 13 per cent were found in sound or fair health; while among those who were not dependent upon charity 64 per cent were still found to be in sound or fair health.

This warranted the Commission to conclude that the radical difference in family connections and physical well-being are largely accountable for the fact that some persons must seek the poorhouse in old age, while others remain presumably non-dependent.

The Commission's findings also disclosed that very few old men remain at work at their habitual occupations. It was found that many of the old had their earning power impaired entirely when reaching old age. Of the almshouse inmates it was found that 73 per cent earned less than $12 per week before they were admitted to the institution. Even among the non-dependent old people 27 per cent had to cease regular work before they had attained the age of 50, while 35 per cent more quit work between the ages of 50 and 60.

Possessions of the Aged

, the property possessions of the aged in Pennsylvania it was
hat but few aged persons in the State are possessed of same.
ve and one-half per cent of the paupers investigated claimed
had property above debts at any time, while of the old persons
State in general 38 per cent claimed to have had some property
· own. SIXTY-TWO PER CENT OF THE LATTER HAD NO
ERTY POSSESSIONS. FURTHERMORE, FORTY-THREE
ENT OF THE AGED POPULATION INVESTIGATED IN
: OWN HOMES HAD NO OTHER MEANS OF SUPPORT
DE THEIR OWN EARNINGS UPON REACHING OLD

The Antiquated Almhouse

)wing the Commission's study of 82 county and local poor-
it concluded that:

"1.   Our poorhouses are organized and maintained on
the principle of charity.

"2·   The heads of these institutions are largely political appointees and very few have had experience in their
work previous to their appointment.

"3·   Many of the men connected with the management of the almhouses are prejudiced against their unfortunate inmates and are often without the rudiments
of an education which would fit them for their responsibilities.

"4·   Life in an almhouse is dull, depressing, restrict-
ed, and to say the least, not an inviting place to spend
one's last days.

"5·   In many county poorhouses the worthy, but unfortunate aged wage earners are compelled, after a life

Food Rations Provided Annually for the Inmates and the Supervisors of a County Almhouse in Pennsylvania.

Articles of Food	Per inmate	Per Stewart
Butter	7½ pounds	30 pounds
Eggs	38	200
Chicken	1 ounce	10 pounds
Milk	23 quarts	101 quarts*

What it Costs to Support an Inmate in an Almhouse

Regarding the accounting system in vogue at that period, the Commission declared that:

"Not only is there no uniform system of accounting and bookkeeping for all the different poor boards' and superintendents' records—which has been a universal practice in all our neighboring States for many years—but even the computations of costs are made in haphazard fashion, in accordance with the desires and best interests of the individuals responsible for the expenditure." ....

"In examining the returned reports, for the year 1917, the commission found it so perplexing that it could make little progress. Only twenty-six of the seventy-three reports submitted for the year 1917 could in any way be made to check. When further inquiry was made of a number of superintendents as to their methods of computation, only about 50 per cent responded. Of all the replies received, each one had his own method showing how the per capita cost per week was obtained."

The Commission's own classification of the costs submitted showed that "THE WEEKLY COST PER INMATE IN 1916 RAN AS HIGH

*The unchangeableness of this order of things is evident from the following story of a Welfare department worker who, last fall, went to a meeting of the Directors of the Poor of one county to ask for some outdoor relief in behalf of an aged couple who have lived in the county over 70 years and who had free rent but no other means.

"After filling out the proper blanks necessary, a representative of the local charity organization and myself went to the meeting of the directors of the poor. We got there a little after ten in the morning but were not admitted until after dinner. At 11:30 we were called to dinner. There were present at the table, the steward, two directors of the poor, one with his son, the solicitor with his mother and a friend of hers, the doctor, the treasurer and a number of other people all together about a dozen persons.

"The table was laden with food of the finest quality. There were two enormous platters of fried spring chicken, representing at least ten or twelve chickens, two platters of boiled ham, huge bowls of mashed potatoes, sweet potatoes, corn, lima beans, large platters of sliced tomatoes, bowls of stewed peaches and spiced peaches, pepper hash, platters of cheese, great platters of bread and cinnamon buns, enormous molds of fresh made butter, cuts of delicious cantaloupes, custard pie and most generous helpings of homemade chocolate ice cream and cocoanut cake, coffee with rich cream.

"After the dinner consultant related the case of the couple and suggested that they grant an allowance of $20 a month, which, with their free rent and their little garden would keep the family in some comfort. This nearly took them off their feet as they declared they 'never grant more than $5.00 a month to any family, no matter what size nor what conditions.'

"The Steward, when asked what their per capita was in the almshouse, said 'about four dollars a week per person.' When consultant pointed out that this would be at least thirty-five dollars a month if they admitted the old couple, they said that would not enter into the question.' They would provide for them in the home to be sure, take them away from the little granddaughter they had reared and who was a great comfort to them, but would not consider under any circumstances granting more than $5.00. They have many couples living on $4.00 a month in great comfort. The Steward said that if they had their rent, clothes and potatoes they would need nothing but bread, and $5.00 a month would buy all the bread they could eat."

LOWEST, TO $16.14 PER WEEK, THE HIGHEST.
RAGE MONTHLY PER CAPITA COST IN 1917 was
IICH IN MOST CASES DID NOT INCLUDE THE
F THE FARM PRODUCTS PRODUCED IN THE ALM-
'ARMS AND CONSUMED BY THE INMATES."

Inadequacy of Other Means of Relief

the Old Age Pension Commission also made an exhaus-
of all the existing means of relief for the aged and found
e extremely inadequate. The Commission found only 20
erns in Pennsylvania which have established regular sys-
nsions for their aged workers. In 1917-18, the total number
in this State in receipt of industrial pensions was 2,052.
number of railroad pensioners in Pennsylvania, during the
)d, was approximately 3,600. Of the nearly 50,000 teachers
te there were only 620 receiving old age pensions in 1918.
m, 852 policemen, 514 firemen and 293 general municipal
were receiving pensions from the various municipalities.
fraternal and trade union organizations in Pennsylvania,
t 100 were receiving old age benefits. The total number of
ers and salaried persons on pensions lists in Pennsyl
1918 hardly reached 10,000 which was less than 3 per cent
'sons 65 years of age and over in the State.

Commission Continued by 1919 Legislature

nmission, in its report to the 1919 Legislature, did not make
te recommendations as to remedial measures to be adopted
; considered its investigations still incomplete and desired
? to complete its studies. It could not, at that time, decide
it would be the best plan to suggest which would warrant
aent into law by the State. It therefore urged further study
)blem.
pliance with this request, the Legislature of 1919 by Joint
n No. 383-A provided for the continuation of the Com-
nd further directed this Commission "to make report and
dations to the General Assembly of One Thousand Nine
and Twenty-one."

Commission's Report, 1921

wo years of exhaustive studies of the various old age pen-
ms abroad, the Commission drafted an old age assistance
ı was introduced in the 1921 Legislature by Senator Max
Speaking of the Leslie bill, the Commission, in its report
?1 Legislature declared:

"In presenting this bill we wish to state that it is our sincere conviction that the problems of the aged can no longer be ignored. We believe that the present time is a proper and propitious one for state action in regard to its old persons. To protect the aged by means of a constructive social policy represents no longer a legislative innovation, nor is it an Utopian experiment. Nearly 30 countries, including all the industrial nations of the world, have already enacted such legislation. Many of these have had such systems for a number of years, and it is important to note that not one nation has as yet returned to the earlier and haphazard methods of individual relief. Indeed, the tendencies in every country are to extend and liberalize the old age protection systems now in operation.

"In proposing a non-contributory assistance system for the Commonwealth of Pennsylvania, we have been guided largely by the experiences of English-speaking countries where this system has been in successful operation for a number of years. A system of compulsory-contributory insurance, while sound in theory and practiced successfully in a number of European countries, involves numerous difficulties—constitutional as well as psychological—which must first be overcome in this country. The cost of bookkeeping and accounting involved in a contributory scheme with the mobility of persons characteristic of such a State as Pennsylvania would doubtless consume most of the income which would be derived from such a plan. The cost of recording the movement and contributions of a citizen of Pennsylvania from his youth till he had reached the age of 65 can hardly be over-estimated. Straight assistance plans are now in existence in the following countries:—Australia, Alaska, Denmark, Great Britain, New Zealand, Uruguay and partly in France. After a thorough study of the various old age insurance systems now in operation, we are convinced that a non-contributory assistance plan is a feasible plan which can be successfully established in Pennsylvania."

CHAPTER IV.

THE OLD AGE ASSISTANCE ACT

The Leslie Bill having made little progress, and the movement for old age pensions for our worthy aged having, meanwhile, gained impetus, the Bill, with only slight changes in its provisions, was re-introduced in the 1923 Legislature by Senator Wm. S. Vare. It was enacted by a vote of 131 against 29 in the House of Representatives and 35 against 9 in the Senate. The Act, with appropriate ceremonies, was signed by Governor Gifford Pinchot on May 10, 1923.

ı years.

Who have been continuous residents of the State of Penn-
ńia for at least fifteen years immediately preceding the date
plication; (continuous residence is not deemed interrupted if
otal period of absence from the State does not exceed three
.) or,

Who have resided in Pennsylvania a total of forty years at
five of which have immediately preceded the application.

Whose income from all sources is below $1.00 per day.

Whose property valuation does not exceed $3,000. (The pro-
· of both husband and wife, when living together, is figured
it were that of one person.)

Who, at the date of application, are not inmates of either
ns, jails, workhouses, insane asylums, or any other public re-
or correctional institution.

} Who, for six months or more, during the fifteen years preced-
he date of application have not deserted their wives or husbands
)ut just cause and failed to support such of their children as
under age.

) Who within the year preceding the application for assistance
not been professional tramps or beggars.

ı · Who have no children or other person responsible for their
ort under the laws of the State and able to do so.

Amount of Assistance

e Act also provides that "the amount of assistance shall be fixed
due regard to the condition in each case, but in no case shall it.
u amount, which, when added to the income of the applicant
all other sources, shall exceed a total of one dollar a day."

How the Law is Administered

e law is administered for the State by a Commission of three
are appointed by the Governor and by local County Old Age
stance Boards who are appointed by the County Commissioners
ich respective county. All members serve without pay except
in the case of the Old Age Assistance Commission each member
.ves as compensation ten dollars per diem while actually engaged
e business of the Commission. All payments for assistance, and
:xpenses incurred by the Commission are paid by the State
surer, while all expenses incurred by the county boards are paid

by the respective county treasurers from the moneys of the county. An appropriation of $25,000 for the two fiscal years was made to the Old Age Assistance Commission by the 1923 Legislature.

Members of Commission

Early in August, 1923, Governor Gifford Pinchot appointed to the Old Age Assistance Commission, Mrs. Mary V. Grice, Philadelphia, Messrs. David S. Ludlum, Ardmore, and James H. Maurer, Reading all members of the previous investigating Commission. At its first meeting on September 6, the Commission appointed Andrew P. Bower, Reading, as Superintendent and Abraham Epstein, Director of Research of the Old Age Pension Commission, as its Executive Secretary.

Early Plans of Commission

The task which faced the Old Age Assistance Commission was not inconsiderable. From the very start, the Commission was confronted with this excellent law and the blessings of the legislature to pay assistance to all our worthy aged, but without any appropriations to accompany these good wishes. Although determined to be as economical as possible, it was, of course, obvious that but little would be left for the payment of assistance after the various county boards had been organized and the machinery established. Still, it was our cherished hope that by practicing the strictest economy we could devote at least some of our meager funds to the actual payment of assistance. In doing so we had hoped to express best not only the letter of the law but also the spirit of the legislature and the wishes of the people of this Commonwealth. However, in view of the proceedings instituted in the Dauphin County Court on February 7, 1924, questioning the constitutionality of the Old Age Assistance Act, these hopes had to be given up early in our work.

What Commission Endeavored To Do.

Prevented from the granting of assistance by the meager appropriations and by the court litigations, we have concentrated all our energies upon establishing the machinery provided under the law in order to ascertain definitely as to the number and character of those who would be entitled to this assistance and the amount this would cost the State. Thuswise, it was our hope to settle once for all, if possible, the mooted question regarding the number of aged persons in Pennsylvania who would qualify under our law and the amount this would cost the State; although, it is obvious that this question could be determined most accurately only after the law had been put in actual and full operation. But we felt that even with all the obstacles facing us we could obtain some estimate of this question which we believe is uppermost in the minds of the legislature and taxpayers.

It is to the carrying out of this task, at least, that we set ourselves most zealously and diligently, and we hope our labors have met with some fruition and our findings will help to shed, at least, some further light upon this great question. We, therefore, submit herewith a summary of our activities and achievements for the period of fifteen months of our existence.

Forty-Five County Boards Organized.

By August 4th, when the Dauphin County Court rendered its decision—only seven months after we were able to ask the County Commissioners to appoint their boards—we succeeded, with the cooperation of the County Commissioners, in organizing Old Age Assistance Boards in the following forty-five counties:—Adams, Beaver, Bedford, Berks, Bradford, Butler, Cambria, Cameron, Centre, Chester, Clarion, Clearfield, Clinton, Columbia, Crawford, Erie, Fayette, Fulton, Greene, Huntingdon, Indiana, Jefferson, Lackawanna, Lawrence, Lycoming, McKean, Mercer, Mifflin, Monroe, Montour, Northumberland, Perry, Pike, Potter, Snyder, Somerset, Sullivan, Susquehanna, Tioga, Union, Venango, Warren, Washington, Westmoreland and York. These required the appointment of 135 persons, all of them recruited from the highest type of citizenship in their respective communities.*

Our staff made over 100 visits into the counties and were in every county except three, while a number of counties were visited more than once, and almost a dozen more were helped in their investigations by our Executive Secretary. Excepting a few counties, the local boards everywhere have been exceedingly active and have given most generously and unselfishly of their time and energies in the promotion of this great cause. Indeed, the amount of unselfish labor rendered by the very busy men and women on our county boards, in the following up of applications and in making their reports, is sufficient to give one renewed hope and faith in the inherent kindness and idealism of our people. Only a just cause could have elicited this genuine support. The response of all these men and women has indeed been most gratifying. Thirty-eight of these county boards which have sent in complete statements, received up to November 1924, a total of 3,347 applications. At a negligible expense to the

*That these Board Members represent a fair cross-section of the various groups in our communities is shown by the following study of the occupations of these men and women. A quest'onaire returned by 91 members shows that 24 are housew'ves: 22 are business men and merchants; 8 are occupying clerical positions; 6 each are teachers and farmers; 4 are physicians; 3 each are recrnited from lawyers, ministers, social workers and salesmen; 2 each are manufacturers, legislators and bankers, while one has already retired, one is an undertaker, and one a laborer. Most of these men and women have held or are now holding various positions of honor in their respective communities.

county, and practically none to the State, these boards have been able to decide definitely upon 2,138 of these applications; the rest still awaiting decision upon further investigation.

Analysis of 2,349 Applications

Of the applications sent in to us for final disposal, after recommendations have been made by the county boards, we have been able to analyze, for the purposes of this report, a total of 2,349 coming from the following 29 counties:—Adams, Beaver, Bedford, Berks, Bradford, Cameron, Centre, Chester, Clearfield, Columbia, Crawford, Fulton, Huntingdon, Indiana, Jefferson, Lycoming, McKean, Mercer, Mifflin, Monroe, Montour, Northumberland, Somerset, Tioga, Union, Venango, Warren, Washington and Westmoreland. While most of these counties are largely rural, there are included a sufficient number of counties that are representative of both the rural and industrial sections of the State to make this study fairly representative of the State's population. Unfortunately, we were unable to include in this summary the two largest counties in the State; no local boards having been organized in either of these counties up to the time of the Dauphin County Court decision. These twenty-nine counties in 1920, had a population of 2,123,516, representing approximately one-fourth of the total population of the State.

How Applications were Secured.

In each county, as soon as a local board was organized, a statement was issued to the press regarding the provisions of the Old Age Assistance Law. All persons who considered themselves qualified under the act were advised to file their applications without delay with the county boards, although mention was made that there would be no money immediately available for the payment of such grants. Applications were made procurable either from the members of the boards directly or from the county commissioners' offices in the respective court houses, which could be obtained in person or by mail. That many aged persons promptly took advantage of this was evidenced by the avalanche of requests for applications immediately following such news releases, and by the further fact that in a number of counties the local boards feel that most of the aged entitled under this law have already filed their applications.

. The 2,349 applications analyzed in this study contain rather detailed and comprehensive data. They have been generally filled out by the applicants themselves giving as references at least two non-relatives; their statements were attested to by an oath before a Notary Public or a Justice of the Peace, and these were further investigated carefully by the County Boards—many of whom in the smaller counties know the applicants personally—before final deci-

)ur executive secretary. From the viewpoint of social
're reliable data was perhaps ever collected, apd the
by these sworn statements are, therefore, of supreme

TABLE I. SEX

TY	TOTAL	MALE		FEMALE	
		No.	Per cent	No.	Per cent
------------------------	79	44	55.7	35	44.3
------------------------	111	59	53.1u	52	46.9
------------------------	97	55	56.7	42	43.3
------------------------	117	59	50.4	58	49.6
------------------------	95	59	62.1	36	37.9
------------------------	26	19	73.1	7	26.9
------------------------	149	88	59.1	61	40.9
------------------------	40	18	45.0	22	55.0
------------------------	253	172	68.0	81	32.0
------------------------	49	25	51.0	24	49.0
------------------------	47	29	51.7	18	38.3
------------------------	31	21	67.7	10	32.3
------------------------	81	53	65.4	28	34.6
------------------------	80	54	67.5	26	32.5
------------------------	131	85	64.9	46	35.1
------------------------	98	69	70.4	29	29.6
------------------------	92	63	68.5	29	31.5
------------------------	57	25	43.9	32	56.1
------------------------	50	28	56.0	22	44.0
------------------------	14	8	57.1	6	42.9
------------------------	22	16	72.7	6	27.3
------------------------	88	50	56.8	38	43.2
------------------------	138	89	64.5	49	35.5
------------------------	80	48	60.0	32	40.0
------------------------	66	45	68.2	21	31.8
------------------------	104	67	64.4	37	35.6
------------------------	64	40	62.5	24	37.5
------------------------	69	46	66.7	23	33.3
------------------------	21	10	47.6	11	52.4
------------------------	2,349	1,444	61.5	905	38.5

rom the above table that of the 2,349 applicants from
ie counties in the State studied· 1,444, or 61.5 per
while 905, or 38.5 per cent, are women. Cameron
nallest in the State, leads in the number of men; the
iting about three-fourths of the applicants of that
Mercer has the lowest percentage of men applicants
ut 43.9 per cent of the total. In general, it appears
exceptions, the number of male applicants are highest
óunties while in the more industrial sections the per-
nen applicants are higher. This may be said to support
.ssertion that women die sooner in rural districts and
industrial centers, but also perhaps indicates that aged
tter provided for in the smaller communities, and that
in industrial occupations can neither hope to live as
in rural counties nor to be as good providers as the
20 U. S. Census also shows that of persons 70 years of
dvania. there were only 103.814 males as against 123.-

of males is 4.2 as against 4.8 of females. This, in spite of the fact that, according to the same census, the number of males for all ages exceeds that of females by over 100,000.

TABLE II. AGES

COUNTY	TOTAL	70 to 74		75 to 79		80 to 84		85 to 89		90 & over	
		No.	Per Cent	No.	Per Cent	No.	Per Cent	No.	Per Cent	No.	Per Cent
Adams,	79	37	46.8	31	39.2	7	8.9	4	5.1	--	--
Beaver,	111	59	53.2	34	30.6	14	12.6	1	0.9	3	2.7
Bedford,	97	53	54.6	32	33.0	10	10.3	2	2.1	--	--
Berks,	117	53	45.3	44	37.6	14	12.0	4	3.4	2	1.7
Bradford,	95	44	46.3	28	29.5	14	14.7	6	6.3	3	3.2
Cameron,	26	15	57.7	4	15.4	4	15.4	1	3.8	2	7.7
Centre,	149	69	46.3	52	34.9	18	12.1	6	4.0	4	2.7
Chester,	40	17	42.5	14	35.0	6	15.0	2	5.0	1	2.5
Clearfield,	253	134	53.0	76	30.0	31	12.3	10	4.0	2	0.7
Columbia,	49	20	40.8	15	30.6	9	18.4	5	10.2	--	--
Crawford,	47	17	36.2	20	42.6	7	14.9	1	2.1	2	4.2
Fulton,	31	19	61.3	10	32.3	1	3.2	1	3.2	--	--
Huntingdon,	81	41	50.6	34	42.0	4	5.0	1	1.2	1	1.2
Indiana,	80	40	50.0	31	38.7	5	6.3	2	2.5	2	2.5
Jefferson,	131	71	54.2	48	36.7	10	7.6	2	1.5	--	--
Lycoming,	98	59	60.2	24	24.5	9	9.2	6	6.1	--	--
McKean,	92	36	39.1	36	39.1	17	18.5	3	3.3	--	--
Mercer,	57	28	49.1	13	22.8	10	17.6	2	3.5	4	7.0
Mifflin,	50	25	50.0	17	34.0	6	12.0	1	2.0	1	2.0
Monroe,	14	6	42.9	4	28.7	2	14.2	1	7.1	1	7.1
Montour,	22	13	59.1	6	27.3	2	9.1	1	4.5	--	--
Northumberland,	88	33	37.5	35	39.8	11	12.5	6	6.8	3	3.4
Somerset,	138	74	53.6	46	33.4	12	8.7	5	3.6	1	.7
Tioga,	80	39	48.8	27	33.7	10	12.5	4	5.0	--	--
Union,	66	32	48.6	19	28.8	11	16.6	3	4.5	1	1.5
Venango,	104	53	51.0	34	32.6	11	10.6	5	4.8	1	1.0
Warren,	64	28	43.8	21	32.8	9	14.1	5	7.8	1	1.5
Washington,	69	33	47.8	23	33.3	8	11.6	5	7.3	--	--
Westmoreland,	21	10	47.6	4	19.1	3	14.3	3	14.3	1	4.7
Total,	2,349	1,158		782		275		98		36	
Average Percentage,			49.5		33.0		12.0		4.0		1.5

The preceding table shows that practically half of the applicants studied are between the ages of 70 to 74, while one-third more are between the ages of 75 and 79 and only less than 18 per cent of the total are 80 years of age and over. Persons of 85 and over constitute less than six per cent, while those of 90 and over amount to less than two per cent. The fact that the percentages are about the same in the rural counties as in the more industrial ones would seem to indicate that, under present conditions, even in the rural communities, by the time the laboring or farming man has reached 70 years of age his ability to earn a livelihood through his own earnings, has, if not entirely ceased, been greatly undermined. The fact that half of the applicants are 75 years of age and over, and have a reduced expectancy of life is important in the consideration of the future responsibilities assumed by the State in the care of these individuals.

MARITAL RELATIONS

Married

Widowed

Single

Legend.

■ U S. 1920 Census of all persons 65 years of age and over.

▣ Applicants of the Old Age Assistance Commission

TABLE III. MARITAL RELATIONS

COUNTY	TOTAL	MARRIED		WIDOWED		SINGLE		SEPARATED	
		No.	Per Cent	No.	Per Cent	No.	Per Cent	No.	Per Cent
Adams, _____	79	25	31.6	38	48.1	15	19.0	1	1.3
Beaver, _____	111	27	24.4	66	59.4	12	10.8	6	5.4
Bedford, _____	97	32	33.0	52	53.6	9	9.3	4	4.1
Berks, _____	117	28	23.9	62	53.0	27	23.1		
Bradford, _____	95	28	29.5	53	55.8	10	10.5	4	4.2
Cameron, _____	26	5	19.3	15	57.7	6	23.0		
Centre, _____	149	46	30.9	75	50.3	23	15.4	5	3.4
Chester, _____	40	16	40.0	20	50.0	3	7.5	1	2.5
Clearfield, _____	253	105	41.5	126	49.8	18	7.1	4	1.6
Columbia, _____	49	10	20.4	32	65.3	6	12.3	1	2.0
Crawford, _____	47	16	34.3	26	55.2	5	10.5		
Fulton, _____	31	12	38.7	14	45.2	5	16.1		
Huntingdon, _____	81	28	34.6	42	51.9	9	11.1	2	2.4
Indiana, _____	80	28	35.0	37	46.3	13	16.2	2	2.5
Jefferson, _____	131	71	54.2	46	35.1	13	9.9	1	0.8
Lycoming, _____	98	33	33.7	56	57.2	7	7.1	2	2.0
McKean, _____	92	33	35.9	49	53.3	7	7.6	3	3.2
Mercer, _____	57	21	36.8	33	58.0	2	3.5	1	1.7
Mifflin, _____	50	16	32.0	25	50.0	7	14.0	2	4.0
Monroe, _____	14	3	21.4	6	42.9	5	35.7		
Montour, _____	22	12	54.5	9	41.0	1	4.5		
Northumberland, __	88	23	26.2	55	62.5	8	9.0	2	2.3
Somerset, _____	138	50	36.2	75	54.4	7	5.0	6	4.4
Tioga, _____	80	30	37.5	40	50.0	10	12.5		
Union, _____	66	29	44.0	31	47.0	3	4.5	3	4.5
Venango, _____	104	39	37.5	46	44.2	16	15.4	3	2.9
Warren, _____	64	21	32.8	37	57.8	6	9.4		
Washington, _____	69	26	37.7	36	52.1	5	7.2	2	3.0
Westmoreland, ____	21	6	28.5	9	42.9	5	23.8	1	4.8
Total, _____	2,349	819	35.0	1,211	51.4	263	11.2	56	2.4

The outstanding features in the above table are the facts that over one-half of the applicants for Old Age Assistance are either widows or widowers, while over one-third are $_{m}$arrie$_{d}$ and still living together. About eleven per cent of the applicants were never married. In view of the fact that the United States Census for 1920 gives the marital relations of all classes, for those 65 years of age and over, in Pennsylvania as 62.4 per cent married and only 29.4 widowed and 7.6 per cent single, the problem of widowhood and lack of family connections as causes of dependency in old age become obvious. In senility, the death of the help-mate and provider—and not infrequently the woman is found to be the provider as well as the man—leaves the poor workman and farmer, or his wife completely helpless and dependent; while the single person having no one to fall back upon for support becomes absolutely dependent as soon as his earnings begin to decline. Striking differences are shown in the proportion of single people in these 29 counties, the percentage ranging from less than 4 per cent in Mercer County, the lowest, to almost 36 per cent in Monroe County. In general, it can be said that the rural counties seem to give a somewhat higher number of single applicants and a lower percentage of widowed persons. Only a little over 2 per cent have their spouses still living but are not residing together—in a few cases it is because the children are unable to maintain them both together, and the old couple are separated and divided up among the children. The problem of maintaining the old in their own homes certainly cannot be ignored, at least, in the case of the widowed, and especially in the case of married couples.

TABLE IV. RESIDING WITH WHOM

County	Total	Family		Alone		Son		Daughter		Relatives		Friends		County Home	
		No.	Per Cent	No.	Per Cent	No.	Per Cent	No.	Per Cent	No.	Per Cent	No.	Per Cent	No.	Per Cent
Adams,	79	26	33.0	15	19.0	9	11.4	16	20.2	12	15.2	1	1.2	----	-----
Beaver,	111	23	20.7	26	23.4	18	16.3	24	21.6	15	13.5	5	4.5	----	-----
Bedford,	97	33	34.0	18	18.6	19	19.6	15	15.5	8	8.2	4	4.1	----	-----
Berks,	117	23	19.7	39	33.3	7	6.0	26	22.2	18	15.3	3	2.6	1	0.9
Bradford,	95	20	21.0	41	43.2	9	9.5	14	14.7	11	11.6	----	-----	----	-----
Cameron,	26	5	19.2	12	46.2	4	15.4	3	11.5	2	7.7	----	-----	----	-----
Centre,	149	40	26.8	45	30.2	22	14.8	21	14.1	17	11.4	4	2.7	----	-----
Chester,	40	11	27.5	8	20.0	2	5.0	9	22.5	10	25.0	----	-----	----	-----
Clearfield,	253	93	36.8	71	28.0	40	15.8	32	12.7	11	4.3	----	-----	6	2.4
Columbia,	49	7	13.7	17	38.0	7	13.7	10	19.0	7	13.7	----	-----	1	1.9
Crawford	47	14	29.7	14	29.7	4	8.5	9	19.3	6	12.8	----	-----	----	-----
Fulton,	31	11	35.5	13	41.9	2	6.5	5	16.1	----	-----	----	-----	----	-----
Huntingdon,	81	25	30.9	28	34.6	8	9.8	12	14.8	6	7.4	----	-----	2	2.5
Indiana,	80	19	23.8	23	28.8	13	16.2	13	16.2	6	7.6	3	3.7	3	3.7
Jefferson,	131	64	48.9	27	20.6	7	5.3	20	15.3	6	4.6	----	-----	7	5.3
Lycoming,	98	26	26.5	28	28.6	13	13.3	23	23.5	8	8.1	----	-----	----	-----
McKean,	92	30	32.6	25	27.2	8	8.7	17	18.5	10	10.9	2	2.1	----	-----
Mercer,	57	15	26.3	7	12.3	10	17.5	14	24.3	10	17.5	1	1.8	----	-----
Mifflin,	50	14	28.0	16	32.0	8	16.0	7	14.0	5	10.0	----	-----	----	-----
Monroe,	14	3	21.4	8	57.1	----	-----	----	-----	2	14.5	1	7.2	----	-----
Montour,	22	12	54.5	6	27.3	1	4.6	3	13.6	----	-----	----	-----	----	-----
Northumberland,	18	14	16.0	22	25.0	13	14.8	16	18.1	21	23.9	1	1.1	1	1.1
Somerset,	138	43	31.1	41	29.7	22	16.0	27	19.5	4	3.0	1	0.7	----	-----
Tioga,	80	28	35.0	28	35.0	8	10.0	6	7.5	10	12.5	----	-----	----	-----
Union,	66	26	39.4	16	24.3	7	10.6	11	16.7	3	4.5	3	4.5	----	-----
Venango,	104	31	29.8	38	31.7	9	8.7	15	14.4	15	14.4	----	-----	1	1.0
Warren,	64	14	21.9	32	50.0	6	9.4	9	14.0	2	3.1	1	1.6	----	-----
Washington,	69	23	33.3	17	24.6	10	14.5	12	17.4	5	7.2	2	3.0	----	-----
Westmoreland,	21	2	9.5	11	52.4	2	9.5	4	19.1	2	9.5	----	-----	----	-----
Total,	2,349	695	29.6	687	29.2	288	12.2	393	16.7	232	9.9	32	1.4	22	1.0

One thousand three hundred and seventy-six of the 2,349, or almost 60 per cent, of the aged applicants in the twenty-nine counties studied continue to reside together either with their wives or with one of their sons or daughters, thus maintaining the family union and indicating that the majority of these aged applicants have homes in which they could be maintained instead of forcing them to break up all their family ties. Over eleven per cent more make their homes with relatives such as brothers and sisters, grand children and unrelated friends who endeavor to help them. The charitableness of some of the latter is indeed marvelous, as instanced in the case of one woman who was supported by an unrelated friend who took in washing for a living. A number of similar conditions were disclosed in many counties. Only about 30 per cent of these applicants reside by themselves or with total strangers. It is interesting to note here that the number of aged applicants who make their homes with their daughters, i. e. sons-in-law, is considerably larger than the number living with their sons, or daughters-in-law. This may perhaps bear out the general belief in the difficulties of aged persons to get along with their daughters-in-law. It is clear also that although sons-in-law are not required to support their dependent aged under our laws, they make every effort to do so, regardless of the hardships involved. Twenty-two of the applicants were already residents of the various county homes.

TABLE V. BIRTH PLACE

COUNTY	TOTAL	IN SAME COUNTY		OTHER COUNTIES IN PENNA.		OTHER STATES		FOREIGN	
		No.	Per Cent	No.	Per Cent	No.	Per Cent	No.	Per Cent
Adams,	79	61	77.2	6	7.6	12	15.2	----	---------
Beaver,	111	57	50.5	16	14.4	17	15.3	21	19.3
Bedford,	97	62	64.0	24	24.7	6	6.2	5	5.1
Berks,	117	77	65.8	26	22.2	6	5.2	8	6.8
Bradford,	95	64	67.4	18	19.0	12	12.6	1	1.0
Cameron,	26	11	42.3	2	7.7	7	27.0	6	23.0
Centre,	149	99	66.4	38	25.5	7	4.7	5	3.4
Chester,	40	27	67.5	11	27.5	1	2.5	1	2.5
Clearfield,	253	145	57.3	45	17.8	8	3.2	55	21.7
Columbia,	49	32	65.3	13	26.5	1	2.1	3	6.1
Crawford,	47	27	57.4	6	12.8	12	25.5	2	4.3
Fulton,	31	24	77.4	4	12.9	3	9.7	----	---------
Huntingdon,	81	53	65.4	24	24.7	1	1.3	7	8.6
Indiana,	80	52	65.0	10	12.5	8	10.0	10	12.5
Jefferson,	131	67	51.2	35	26.7	3	2.3	26	19.8
Lycoming,	98	52	53.1	25	25.5	11	11.2	10	10.2
McKean,	92	19	20.7	30	32.6	35	39.0	8	8.7
Mercer,	57	25	43.9	17	29.8	6	10.5	9	15.8
Mifflin,	50	34	68.0	16	32.0	----	---------	----	---------
Monroe,	14	11	78.7	1	7.1	1	7.1	1	7.1
Montour,	22	13	59.1	7	31.8	2	9.1	----	---------
Northumberland,	88	45	51.1	28	31.8	4	4.6	11	12.5
Somerset,	138	90	65.2	27	19.6	11	8.0	10	7.2
Tioga,	80	49	61.3	12	15.0	18	22.5	1	1.2
Union,	66	41	62.1	21	31.8	3	4.6	1	1.5
Venango,	104	67	64.4	26	25.0	5	4.8	6	5.8
Warren,	64	33	51.6	9	14.0	14	21.9	8	12.5
Washington,	69	26	37.7	16	23.2	12	17.4	15	21.7
Westmoreland,	21	11	52.4	6	28.6	----	---------	4	19.0
Total,	2,349	1,374	58.5	515	22.0	226	9.5	234	10.0

Birthplace

That the problem of old age dependency in Pennsylvania native one is strikingly borne out by our examination of these cations. Of the 2,349 applications summarized, 2,115, or 90 pe of the total were born in the United States; 58.5 per cent of were born in the same county, while 22 per cent more were within the State and 10 per cent in other states. There we foreign born applicants in Adams, Fulton, Mifflin and Mc counties while Bradford, Chester, Monroe, Tioga and Union co each had but one applicant of foreign birth. Beaver, Can Clearfield, Jefferson and Washington counties with their hig centages of foreign born gave the largest number; but in no c does the number exceed 23 per cent of the total applications received.

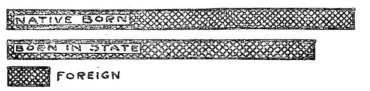

BIRTHPLACE OF APPLICANT

NATIVE BORN

BORN IN STATE

FOREIGN

Nearly 53 per cent of those born abroad came from En Scotland and Wales; 14 per cent came from Germany; 12 pe from Ireland; 8 per cent from the Scandinavian countries persons from all other countries combined constituted about cent of the total. The percentages of the newer immigrants Southern and Eastern Europe do not exceed 3 per cent of the This, of course, is largely explained by the fact that the im tion from the latter countries is of comparatively recent dat most immigrants come here in the prime of life they could not ally come under the age limit imposed by the Old Age Assi Act. It is also important to note that excepting a negligible n practically all of the foreign born, as well as those from other have resided in Pennsylvania for at least a period of thirty yea more—a great many more than 50 years—thus establishing the claim for some help in their declining days, when they are no able to eke out an existence, from the Commonwealth for prosperity and development they have labored and toiled a which they have paid taxes during a lifetime.

TABLE VI. DISABILITIES

County	Total	Old Age No.	Old Age Per Cent	Rheumatism No.	Rheumatism Per Cent	Asthma No.	Asthma Per Cent	Loss of Arms, Legs & Eyes No.	Loss of Arms, Legs & Eyes Per Cent	Blind & Deaf No.	Blind & Deaf Per Cent	Rupture No.	Rupture Per Cent	Paralysis No.	Paralysis Per Cent	Miscellaneous No.	Miscellaneous Per Cent	None No.	None Per Cent	Not Stated No.	Not Stated Per Cent
Adams,	79	26	33.0	8	10.1	2	2.5	4	5.1	4	5.0	3	3.8	3	3.8	17	21.5	5	6.3	7	8.9
Beaver,	111	34	30.6	16	14.5	3	2.7			7	6.3	4	3.6	9	8.1	16	14.4			22	19.8
Bedford,	97	38	39.2	4	4.1	6	6.2	8	8.2	4	4.1	4	4.1	6	6.2	7	7.3	1	1.0	19	19.6
Berks,	117	33	28.2	9	7.7	1	0.9	4	3.4	5	4.3	2	1.7	4	3.4	16	13.7			43	36.7
Bradford,	95	29	30.5	14	14.7			8	8.4	8	8.4	4	4.2	3	3.2	13	13.7	1	3.8	16	16.9
Cameron,	26	10	38.5	5	19.2			5	19.2	1	3.8									4	15.5
Centre,	149	44	29.5	15	10.1	3	2.0	7	4.7	12	8.0	5	3.4	4	2.7	30	20.1	1	3.2	29	19.5
Chester,	40	12	30.0			1	2.5	3	7.5	2	5.0	2	5.0	3	7.5		20.0			9	22.5
Clearfield,	253	89	35.2	28	11.1	8	3.2	34	13.4	11	4.3	12	4.7	12	4.7	15	6.0	8	3.2	36	14.2
Columbia,	49	18	36.7	8	16.3					2	4.8					9	18.4			9	18.4
Crawford,	47	13	27.7	6	12.8	3	6.4	8	17.0	4	8.2	1	2.1			1	2.1	1	2.1	9	19.1
Fulton,	31	11	35.5	5	16.1	1	1.2	11	13.6	3	6.4	4	6.5	1	2.0	3	9.7	1	3.2	8	25.8
Huntingdon,	81	28	34.6	11	13.6	2	2.5	10	12.5	3	3.2	7	5.0	2	4.3	6	7.4	2	1.2	11	13.6
Indiana,	80	24	30.0	11	13.7	7	5.3	19	14.5	2	2.5	5	8.7			5	6.3	4	2.5	16	20.0
Jefferson,	131	49	37.4	20	15.3	2	2.0	7	7.2	10	7.6	10	3.8	5	6.2	6	4.6	4	3.1	4	3.1
Lycoming,	98	35	35.7	18	18.4			9	9.8			10	10.2	1	1.3	9	9.2	4	4.1	12	12.2
McKean,	92	26	28.2	11	12.0	2	4.0	4	7.0	5	5.4	9	9.8	4	5.3	17	18.5			11	12.0
Mercer,	57	21	36.8	3	3.6			3	6.0	6	10.5			2	3.5	7	12.3			15	26.3
Mifflin,	50	17	34.0	6	12.0			1	2.0	1	2.0	3	6.0	3	6.0	5	10.0	4	8.0	6	12.0
Monroe,	14	2	14.3	4	28.6			6	27.2	1	7.1					2	14.3			4	28.6
Montour,	22	4	18.9	4	18.2			3	3.4							4	18.2	1	4.6	3	13.6
Northumberland,	88	28	31.8	10	11.4	3	3.4	14	10.1	5	5.7	1	1.1	2	2.3	12	13.6	13	14.8	11	12.5
Somerset,	138	44	31.9	31	22.5	11	8.0	9	11.3	1	0.8	2	1.4	5	3.6	14	10.1	3	2.2	13	9.4
Tioga,	80	20	25.0	5	6.3	6	7.5	3	4.5	7	8.7	7	8.7				8.7	5	6.3	14	17.5
Union,	66	15	22.8	8	12.1	1	1.5	8	11.5	1	1.5	8	10.6	6	9.1	13	19.7	3	1.5	11	16.7
Venango,	104	30	28.8	24	23.1	1	1.0	12	14.1	5	4.8	1	0.7	5	4.8	7	9.7	3	2.9	9	8.7
Warren,	64	6	23.4	6	9.4	1	3.1	9	14.1	2	11.0	1	7.7	5	3.1	7	6.2	8	12.5	10	15.6
Washington,	69	16	23.2	15	21.7	3	3.1	2	3.0	1	1.4	1	1.6	5	4.8	11	15.9	4	2.9	8	11.6
Westmoreland,	21	9	42.8	2	9.5	4	5.8	3	14.3	1	4.8	5	7.2	3	4.4	3	14.3		5.8	3	14.3
Total,	2,349	740	31.5	306	13.0	69	3.0	206	8.8	118	5.0	108	4.6	93	4.0	267	11.3	70	3.0	372	15.8

Disabilities

Less than one-fifth of the applicants studied failed to design
some special disability; and only three per cent of the total de
itely stated that they had no disability. which either prevented th
from securing permanent employment, or which made it diffic
for them to secure even temporary work of any sort. FOUR O
OF EVERY FIVE APPLICANTS WERE ALREADY EITH
FULLY OR PARTIALLY DISABLED TO AN EXTENT TH
THEIR INCOME FROM EARNINGS WAS EITHER CONSIDI
ABLY REDUCED OR TOTALLY ELIMINATED. Among
causes of indigency assigned by these aged applicants, infirmit
due to old age, lead. The latter have been given exclusively
almost one-third of the applicants as the cause of their incapaci
Next in proportion as causes of physical decline follow rheun
tism, assigned as the leading cause of disability by thirteen per ce
loss of eye, arm or leg 8.8 per cent; blind and deaf, 5 per ce
paralytic afflictions, 4 per cent; asthma, 3 per cent, while over
per cent assigned various troubles which incapacitated them fr
continued employment. The close relationship of old age depe
ency to physical incapacity is thus obvious and needs no comme

TABLE VII. PRESENT OCCUPATIONS.

County	Total	None		Laborer		Housewife		Farmer		Skilled; Semi-Skilled and Clerical		Miscellaneous
		No.	Per Cent	No.	Per Cent	No.	Per Cent	No.	Per Cent	No.	Per Cent	No.
Adams	79	57	72.1	7	8.9	9	11.4	3	3.8	----	----	3
Beaver	11	78	70.3	9	8.1	15	13.5	4	3.6	2	1.8	3
Bedford	97	68	70.1	12	12.4	13	13.4	1	1.0	1	1.0	2
Berks	117	88	75.2	13	11.2	12	10.3	1	0.8	1	0.8	2
Bradford	95	67	70.5	2	2.1	20	21.1	6	6.3	----	----	-
Cameron	26	19	73.1	2	7.7	2	7.7	3	11.5	----	----	-
Center	149	110	73.8	19	12.8	13	8.7	4	2.7	1	0.7	2
Chester	40	29	72.5	1	2.5	8	20.0	----	----	----	----	2
Clearfield	253	196	77.5	21	8.3	18	7.1	6	2.3	4	1.6	8
Columbia	49	35	71.4	7	14.3	4	8.2	----	----	1	2.0	2
Crawford	47	34	72.4	3	6.3	6	12.8	3	6.3	----	----	1
Fulton	31	17	54.8	6	19.4	6	19.4	1	3.2	1	3.2	----
Huntingdon	81	58	71.6	8	9.9	15	18.5	----	----	----	----	-
Indiana	80	63	78.8	8	10.0	5	6.3	2	2.5	1	1.2	1
Jefferson	131	88	67.2	14	10.7	17	13.0	5	3.8	3	2.3	4
Lycoming	98	75	76.5	11	11.2	8	8.2	1	1.0	1	1.0	2
McKean	92	66	71.7	10	10.9	13	14.1	2	2.2	----	----	1
Mercer	57	41	72.0	1	1.8	9	15.8	3	5.2	----	----	3
Mifflin	50	38	76.0	8	16.0	3	6.0	----	----	1	2.0	-
Monroe	14	9	64.3	2	14.3	3	21.4	----	----	----	----	-
Montour	22	13	59.1	7	31.9	1	4.5	1	4.5	----	----	-
Northumberland	88	75	85.2	6	6.8	4	4.6	2	2.3	----	----	1
Somerset	138	109	80.0	12	8.7	9	6.5	2	1.5	----	----	6
Tioga	80	46	57.5	15	18.8	4	5.0	6	7.5	2	2.5	7
Union	66	46	69.8	9	13.6	9	13.6	1	1.5	1	1.5	-
Venango	104	76	73.1	15	14.4	10	9.6	----	----	1	1.0	2
Warren	64	32	50.0	12	18.7	11	17.2	5	7.8	3	4.7	1
Washington	69	52	75.3	6	8.7	2	3.0	9	13.0	----	----	-
Westmoreland	21	14	66.6	1	4.8	4	19.0	----	----	1	4.8	1
Total	2,349	1,699	72.3	247	10.5	253	10.8	71	3.0	54	2.3	25

The extent and seriousness of these disabilities when related to modern industry, which requires full vigor and strength, is illustrated further by the fact that, as shown in the preceding table, of the 2,349 applicants in these, mostly rural counties, 1,699, or over 72 per cent, are already without any occupation and thus prevented from continuing the work in which they were engaged a lifetime.

PRESENT OCCUPATIONS

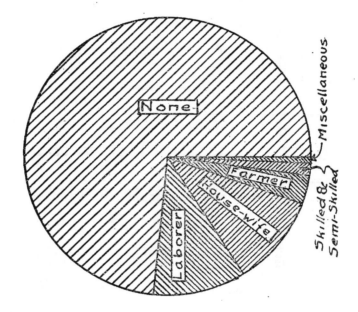

Of those still claiming employment, 11 per cent are women who are merely continuing to do their own house work; only 10.5 per cent are still working on various common labor jobs and are endeavoring to eke out an existence; while 3 per cent are still engaged as farmers or farm laborers. In the entire total of 2,349 applicants only 54 stated that they still continue in the skilled or clerical occupations. The other few are employed to some extent in miscellaneous ways, mainly in performing odd jobs at irregular intervals.

The facts revealed in the following table show conclusively that the problem of old age dependency today is an outgrowth of our industrial expansion with the pace and speed of which the superannuated worker cannot keep up. It also reveals that poverty in old age is directly and intimately related to the poor jobs and inadequate pay of a lifetime. The industrial responsibility for modern dependency in old age is obvious and cannot be shifted. To talk about thriftlessness and shiftlessness, regardless of an inquiry into the jobs held and wages received by these aged persons,

County	Total	Housewife No.	Per Cent	Laborer No.	Per Cent	Farmer No.	Per Cent	Building Trade No.	Per Cent	Miner No.	Per Cent	Skilled Semi-skilled Clerical No.	Per Cent	Professional and Merchant No.	Per Cent	Miscellaneous No.	Per Cent
Adams	79	22	27.8	31	39.2	11	14.0	6	7.6							9	11.4
Beaver	111	34	30.6	36	32.5	4	8.6	7	6.3	2	1.8	22	19.8	2	1.8	4	3.6
Bedford	97	36	37.0	33	34.0	9	9.5	7	7.2	8	8.2	4	4.1			8	6.8
Berks	117	43	36.8	41	35.0	3	2.6	6	5.1			16	13.7	2	2.1	3	8.3
Bradford	95	28	29.5	34	35.8	9	9.5	7	7.4			7	7.4	1	3.8	5	3.8
	26	6	23.0	11	42.5	5	9.2	2	7.7								3.4
Centre	149	49	33.0	50	33.6	18	12.0	9	6.0	3	2.0	15	10.0	1	2.5	1	0.5
	40	17	42.5	10	25.0	2	5.0	2	5.0			8	20.0	4	1.6		
Clearfield	253	58	22.9	80	31.6	37	14.6	18	7.1	44	17.4	11	4.3	3	6.4	9	18.4
	49	13	26.5	16	32.7	3	6.1	2	4.1			6	12.2	1	3.2	3	6.4
Crawford	47	14	29.8	6	12.8	14	29.8	5	10.5			2	4.3			1	3.2
Fulton	31	10	33.1	9	29.0	8	26.0	2	6.5	4	5.0	4	5.0	1	1.2	2	2.5
Huntingdon	61	25	30.8	28	34.6	11	13.5	7	8.6	5	6.2	9	11.2	4	3.1	3	3.8
Indiana	80	19	23.8	27	33.8	10	12.5	6	7.5	15	11.5	12	9.2			3	2.0
Jefferson	131	36	27.5	34	26.0	15	11.5	12	9.2			8	8.2	2	2.2	10	0.2
Lycoming	98	19	19.4	47	48.0	10	10.2	4	4.0			9	9.8			2	2.2
McKean	92	24	26.0	33	35.9	14	15.2	8	8.7	1	1.5	8	5.3			2	3.5
	57	27	47.4	17	30.0	4	7.0	3	5.3			8	16.0	1	2.0	2	4.0
Mifflin	50	15	30.0	19	38.0	2	6.0	2	4.0								
Monroe	14	6	42.9	6	42.9	2	14.2	1	4.5	4	4.6	2	9.1	1	4.5	2	9.1
Montour	22	2	9.1	12	54.6	6	9.1	9	10.2	20	14.5	11	12.5	1	1.1	2	2.3
Northumberland	88	29	33.0	26	29.5	11	6.8	7	5.0	1	1.2	7	5.0	1	0.7	1	67
Somerset	138	49	35.5	42	30.6	24	8.0	5	6.3			4	5.0			7	8.7
Tioga	80	24	30.0	15	18.8	12	30.0	6	9.1	2	1.9	8	12.1				
Union	66	15	22.7	25	38.0	13	18.1	3	2.9			17	16.3	3	2.9	2	1.9
Venango	104	30	28.8	34	32.7	13	12.5	4	6.3			6	9.4	2	3.1	1	1.5
Warren	64	14	21.9	24	37.5	13	20.3										

is merely to dodge the issue. The truth, as shown by these affidavits, is that most of these aged folks have had a life-struggle to make both ends meet in order to maintain themselves as decent and honest citizens. Savings for old age under these conditions were inconceivable! Of the 2,349 applications examined, 781, or one-third, were engaged at the time of ceasing employment in occupations generally classified as common labor; 685, or 29 per cent more, were housewives who have always depended upon the support of their husbands, the latter of whom are now either dead or so disabled as to be unable to maintain them; almost 12 per cent were poor farmers, or more correctly, farm laborers, whose earnings were never sufficient to maintain them even in the commonest decencies; 6.6 per cent were engaged in the building trades, most of them prior to the introduction of the present higher scales paid these workers, while about 5.4 per cent more were engaged in mining coal. Hardly 9 per cent were engaged in what could be termed skilled, semi-skilled or clerical occupations. On the other hand one and one-half per cent were formerly in the professions and business. Indeed, the whimsical turns of fate are indicated further by the fact that in our files we also have applications from a number of professional people such as doctors, teachers, politicians, merchants and persons of well-to-do families against whom destiny has turned, and who, through some misfortune, have lost their all and are now dependent.

TABLE IX. WAGES EARNED AT PRESENT.

. County	Total	None		$1 to 4		$5 to 7		Over $7		Not Stated	
		No.	Per cent	No.	Per cent	No.	Per cent	No.	Per cent	No.	Per cent
Adams	79	67	84.8	10	12.7			2	2.5		
Beaver	111	96	86.5	10	9.0	3	2.7	2	1.8		
Bedford	97	82	84.5	9	9.3	1	1.1	5	5.1		
Berks	117	102	87.2	10	8.5	3	2.6	2	1.7		
Bradford	95	82	86.3	8	8.4	1	1.1	4	4.2		
Cameron	26	22	84.6	3	11.5					1	3.9
Centre	149	127	85.2	14	9.4	3	2.0	5	3.4		
Chester	40	36	90.0	3	7.5	1	2.5				
Clearfield	253	223	88.1	13	5.1	11	4.4	4	1.6	2	0.8
Columbia	49	34	69.4	6	12.2	1	2.1	8	16.3		
Crawford	47	45	95.7							2	4.3
Fulton	31	25	80.5	2	6.5	2	6.5	2	6.5		
Huntingdon	81	67	82.7	9	11.1	3	3.7			2	2.5
Indiana	80	63	78.7	6	7.5	4	5.0	4	5.0	3	3.8
Jefferson	131	118	90.1	9	6.9	3	2.3	1	0.7		
Lycoming	98	77	78.6	9	9.2	1	1.0	11	11.2		
McKean	92	82	89.1	6	6.5	1	1.1	3	3.3		
Mercer	57	53	93.0	3	5.3	1	1.7				
Mifflin	50	41	82.0	6	12.0			3	6.0		
Monroe	14	12	85.7			2	14.3				
Montour	22	15	68.2	5	22.7			2	9.1		
Northumberland	88	81	92.1	4	4.5	2	2.3	1	1.1		
Somerset	138	121	87.7	11	8.0	1	0.7	1	0.7	4	2.9
Tioga	80	60	75.0	12	15.0	1	1.3			7	8.7
Union	66	58	87.9	7	10.6	1	1.5				
Venango	104	89	85.5	8	7.7	1	1.0	3	2.9	3	2.9
Warren	64	47	73.4	8	12.5	2	3.1	4	6.3	3	4.7
Washington	69	65	94.2	2	3.0	1	1.4	1	1.4		
Westmoreland	21	17	81.0	3	14.3					1	4.7
Total	2,349	2,007	85.4	196	8.3	50	2.1	68	3.0	28	1.2

TABLE X. WAGES EARNED WHEN STOPPED WORKING

County	Total	$1 to 9		$10 to 14		$15 to 19		$20 to 24		$25 to 29		$30 & over	
		No.	Per Cent	No.	Per Cent	No.	Per Cent	No.	Per Cent	No.	Per Cent	No.	Per Cent
Adams	48	29	60.4	11	22.9	8	16.7	---	---	---	---	---	---
Beaver	67	18	26.8	14	20.9	16	23.9	9	13.4	8	12.0	2	3.0
Bedford	50	24	48.0	12	24.0	11	22.0	1	2.0	---	---	2	4.0
Berks	63	20	31.7	24	38.1	14	22.2	5	8.0	---	---	---	---
Bradford	59	30	50.8	17	28.8	9	15.3	3	5.1	---	---	---	---
Cameron	20	4	20.0	7	35.0	6	30.0	3	15.0	---	---	---	---
Centre	73	38	52.1	17	23.3	12	16.4	3	4.1	3	4.1	---	---
Chester	23	6	26.1	8	34.8	6	26.1	3	13.0	---	---	---	---
Clearfield	157	47	30.0	37	23.6	40	25.5	20	12.7	11	7.0	2	1.2
Columbia	22	8	36.4	8	36.4	4	18.1	2	9.1	---	---	---	---
Crawford	27	12	44.4	8	29.6	5	18.5	2	7.5	---	---	---	---
Fulton	12	12	100.0	---	---	---	---	---	---	---	---	---	---
Huntingdon	50	26	52.0	10	20.0	9	18.0	5	10.0	---	---	---	---
Indiana	46	22	47.8	8	17.4	7	15.2	6	13.1	2	4.3	1	2.2
Jefferson	79	31	39.2	18	22.8	16	20.2	10	12.7	3	3.8	1	1.3
Lycoming	59	21	35.6	13	22.0	13	22.0	9	15.3	2	3.4	1	1.7
McKean	57	11	19.3	17	29.8	14	24.6	12	21.1	3	5.2	---	---
Mercer	25	7	28.0	5	20.0	6	24.0	4	16.0	3	12.0	---	---
Mifflin	35	15	42.9	11	31.4	5	14.3	2	5.7	2	5.7	---	---
Monroe	6	3	50.0	2	33.3	---	---	1	16.7	---	---	---	---
Montour	16	6	37.5	6	37.5	4	25.0	---	---	---	---	---	---
Northumberland	55	13	23.6	16	29.1	13	23.6	8	14.6	3	5.5	2	3.6
Somerset	78	33	42.3	24	30.8	18	23.1	3	3.8	---	---	---	---
Tioga	32	9	28.1	11	34.4	8	25.0	2	6.3	1	3.1	1	3.1
Union	34	13	38.2	14	41.2	3	8.8	2	5.9	2	5.9	---	---
Venango	60	17	28.3	15	25.0	14	23.4	11	18.3	1	1.7	2	3.3
Warren	35	13	37.1	12	34.3	8	22.8	1	2.9	1	2.9	---	---
Washington	46	10	21.7	8	17.4	14	30.4	7	15.2	6	13.1	1	2.2
Westmoreland	13	7	53.8	21	15.4	1	17.7	13	23.1	---	---	---	---
Total	1,347	505	37.5	355	26.4	284	21.0	137	10.2	49	3.6	17	1.3

As apparent from the two preceding tables, the data brought out in the foregoing discussions are further corroborated by the statements of these applicants regarding their earnings at the time of filing their applications and when they stopped working. Although, as already seen, over 60 per cent of these applicants are under 75 years of age, 85 PER CENT OF THESE AGED PERSONS WERE ALREADY WITHOUT ANY EARNINGS AT THE TIME OF MAKING APPLICATION. Of the less than 15 per cent still claiming some earnings, over 8 per cent eke out less than $4.00 a week, and only 3 per cent earn from $7.00 a week and over —whose claims, in accordance with the law, have been rejected.

WAGES EARNED AT PRESENT

NONE

$1 TO $4

$5 AND OVER

Of the 1,347 applicants who stated the amount of their earnings at the time when they stopped working we find that 37.5 PER CENT EARNED LESS THAN $10 A WEEK, WHILE ALMOST

-THIRDS OF THE TOTAL EARNED AN AVERAGE WAGE
.ESS THAN $15 A WEEK. Only about 5 per cent of these
cants claim to have earned wages in excess of $25 per week.
nuch, as many of these men and women were compelled to
work years before they reached their 70th year, it is evident
even if they had accumulated some meager savings in their
ɛr years, it did not take long to have that "eaten up." In
of these facts, it is indeed ludicrous to accuse these people of
rovidence" and "gross negligence" to provide for their old age.
as absurd is it to claim that for these people the "dread and
ehension of 'over the hill to the poor house' may be a needed
ilus to a self-respecting, thrifty life."

Families of Applicants

the pitifully small wages earned by these people together with
· physical afflictions were not sufficient proof of the inability,
·r present conditions, of these superannuated men and women
rovide themselves with funds for their declining days—when
no longer are able to face the hard struggles of our industrial
d—the excellent character and hard-working propensities of
ɛ applicants are attested further by the following facts:
: the 2,349 persons studied, 89 per cent have been married and
ɛd families, sometimes of as many as 10 and more children. In
respective counties the average number of children still living
applicant ranges from two in Westmoreland to five in Adams,
e the average for all counties studied amounts to 3.7 children
applicant. Inasmuch as these are the children now living,
ɛ obvious that the families actually reared have been much
ɛr, for many an aged person reports of raising 10 or 12 children
·hom only 2 or 3 are now living. Thus, on a wage which, at

The data obtained regarding the children of these applic: of supreme significance not only in shedding light upon the cl ability to support their parents, which is required by law, upon casting a new light upon our entire social structure. of the fact that 90 per cent of these applicants are native b 80 per cent were born in Pennsylvania, the facts disclosed b exceedingly illuminating:

The 2,349 applicants, in the 29 counties studied, stated t have a total of 6,581 children living. The percentages of s daughters were about the same. Sixty-eight per cent children are residing in the same county as their parents, cent live in other counties in the state while about 14 moved to other states. Although the percentage is not ver the fact that the whereabouts of 185 children, constitutin 3 per cent of the total, were unknown to their aged paren say the least, an important social phenomenon. Of the children, 5,288, or over 80 per cent, were already married v siderable families of their own—the average number children being 3.3 per family—;five and one-half per cent children were widows or widowers while only 11 per c still single. and presumably best able to help support their

Occupations of Children of Applicants

Even more significant are the occupations of the children applicants. Of the total number of children, 30.5 per c engaged in common labor occupations; about 9 per cent e miners, farmers, or farm laborers and housewives, whil cent more were engaged in railroads and 3 per cent in the trades; another 3 per cent were holding clerical positio a similar percentage were either disabled or dependant case, it is disclosed that not only do the sons of a laborer or miner follow the father's occupation, but, in the majority of cases, even all his daughters marry people in the same occupations. Frequently, a person with six or eight children classifies them all either as laborers or as married to laborers. The stability of these families is indicated by the strikingly large proportion of these children who continue to reside within the same county. The migration of children to other states is indeed surprisingly low in the counties examined. Again, the fact that nearly one-fourth of the men applicants and over one-third of the women applicants have no children living at all would seem a sufficient answer to the argument that this act would remove the responsibility of the support of parents by their children.

TABLE XI. WHO HELPS TO SUPPORT YOU

County	Total	None		Children		Relatives		County		Friends		Miscellaneous	
		No.	Per Cent	No.	Per Cent	No.	Per Cent	No.	Per Cent	No.	Per Cent	No.	Per Cent
Adams	79	24	30.4	33	41.8	8	10.2	6	7.6	4	5.0	4	5.0
Beaver	111	35	31.5	57	51.4	14	12.6	3	2.7	2	1.8	----	----
Bedford	97	33	34.0	37	38.2	7	7.2	2	2.0	5	5.2	13	13.4
Berks	117	34	29.1	37	31.7	15	12.8	8	6.8	15	12.8	8	6.8
Bradford	95	39	41.0	26	27.4	11	11.6	5	5.2	7	7.4	7	7.4
Cameron	26	9	34.7	7	27.0	1	3.8	3	11.5	5	19.2	1	3.8
Centre	149	41	27.5	56	37.6	21	14.1	7	4.7	17	11.4	7	4.7
Chester	40	13	32.5	12	30.0	10	25.0	----	----	3	7.5	2	5.0
Clearfield	253	99	39.2	98	38.7	12	4.7	24	9.5	11	4.3	9	3.6
Columbia	49	10	20.4	17	34.7	8	16.3	2	4.0	3	6.2	9	18.4
Crawford	47	12	25.5	21	44.7	6	12.8	----	----	3	6.4	5	10.6
Fulton	31	18	58.1	10	32.3	----	----	2	6.4	1	3.2	----	----
Huntingdon	81	25	30.9	31	38.2	8	9.9	10	12.3	3	3.7	4	5.0
Indiana	80	33	41.3	30	37.5	7	8.7	6	7.5	3	3.7	1	1.3
Jefferson	131	60	45.8	48	36.6	5	3.8	14	10.7	4	3.1	----	----
Lycoming	98	43	43.9	37	37.8	6	6.1	3	3.0	----	----	9	9.2
McKean	92	32	34.8	34	37.0	10	10.9	6	6.5	5	5.4	5	5.4
Mercer	57	20	36.1	29	50.9	7	12.3	1	1.7	----	----	----	----
Mifflin	50	17	34.0	19	38.0	5	10.0	1	2.0	2	4.0	6	12.0
Monroe	14	5	35.7	----	----	3	21.4	3	21.4	2	14.3	1	7.2
Montour	22	11	50.0	8	36.4	----	----	----	----	3	13.6	----	----
Northumberland	88	25	28.5	30	35.0	12	13.6	10	11.4	5	5.7	6	6.8
Somerset	138	47	34.0	57	41.3	12	8.7	8	5.8	8	5.8	6	4.4
Tioga	80	30	37.5	22	27.5	8	10.0	4	5.0	6	7.5	10	12.5
Union	66	28	42.5	23	34.8	1	1.6	7	10.6	4	6.0	3	4.5
Venango	104	40	38.5	35	33.6	15	14.4	1	1.0	7	6.7	6	5.8
Warren	64	30	46.9	20	31.2	3	4.7	5	7.8	4	6.3	2	3.1
Washington	69	18	26.0	31	44.9	13	18.8	1	1.5	4	5.8	2	3.0
Westmoreland	21	11	52.3	6	28.6	1	4.8	1	4.8	2	9.5	----	----
Total	2,349	842	35.8	871	37.0	229	9.8	143	6.1	138	5.9	126	5.4

That in spite of their own poverty, the children of these applicants make every effort to support their parents, is borne out by the fact that in 37 per cent of the total cases investigated, the children constitute the sole support of their parents, while 10 per cent more are helped by their relatives, such as brothers and sisters, and grandchildren. One hundred and forty-three applicants, or 6 per cent of the total, are already receiving support from their county or local poor districts; six per cent more are assisted by non-relatives while a little over 5 per cent more are helped through miscellaneous sources. Over 35 per cent are receiving no help from any one.

TABLE XII. HOME OWNERSHIP AND POSSESSIONS OF APPLICANTS

County	Total No. Applicants	Home Owners		Average Value of Home	Possessing Savings		Average Amount of Savings
		No.	Per Cent		No.	Per Cent	
Adams	79	20	25.3	$523	18	22.8	$480
Beaver	111	15	13.5	1,026	21	18.9	445
Bedford	97	29	29.9	603	7	7.2	269
Berks	117	14	11.9	667	21	18.0	394
Bradford	95	41	43.2	400	1	1.0	178
Cameron	26	8	30.7	471	4	15.3	275
Centre	149	30	20.2	421	16	10.7	314
Chester	40	6	15.0	818	12	30.0	416
Clearfield	253	72	28.4	318	46	18.1	531
Columbia	49	9	18.4	262	9	18.4	300
Crawford	47	13	27.6	593	12	25.5	323
Fulton	31	12	38.7	293	5	16.1	249
Huntingdon	81	20	24.7	307	11	13.6	202
Indiana	80	10	12.5	1,333	21	26.3	463
Jefferson	131	49	37.4	424	23	17.6	244
Lycoming	98	14	14.3	545	12	12.2	498
McKean	92	19	20.6	334	7	7.6	527
Mercer	57	15	26.3	617	13	22.8	499
Mifflin	50	16	32.0	689	5	10.0	444
Monroe	14	1	7.2	1,000	5	35.7	642
Montour	22	4	18.2	650	3	13.6	150
Northumberland	88	12	13.6	658	25	28.4	419
Somerset	138	44	31.8	432	24	17.4	330
Tioga	80	18	22.5	688	11	13.7	465
Union	66	25	37.8	648	28	42.4	395
Venango	104	1	1.0	317	25	24.0	190
Warren	64	5	7.8	330	14	21.9	298
Washington	69	13	18.8	947	16	23.2	655
Westmoreland	21	5	23.8	645	7	33.3	835
Total Average	2,349	540	23.0	$571	422	18.0	$376

HOME OWNERSHIP

The utter dependency of these aged applicants is brought out further by the fact that 1.733, or 73.8 per cent, of the 2,349 applicants stated that aside from what help some of them receive from their children and relatives, many of whom have to skimp a great deal in order to do so, they have no other means of support except what they can earn from their own labor. And, as already pointed out, over 85 per cent of the applicants were already not earning anything at the time of filing their applications. Only 422, or 18 per cent, of the total claim to derive some income from accumulated savings. The average of these savings amounted to $376.00 for the persons having such, and $6.75 for all applicants. EVEN IN THESE OVERWHELMINGLY RURAL COUNTIES ONLY LESS THAN ONE-FOURTH OF THE APPLICANTS HAVE BEEN ABLE, DURING THEIR LIFETIME, TO SAVE UP EVEN A HOMESTEAD. This against a home ownership of 44.9 per cent for the entire state, although but little over one-half of these are entirely free. The difficulties of accomplishing that feat are indicated by the fact that the average assessed value of the homestead amounts to but $571.00. The average total possessions of all applicants, including the values of the homes, savings and various other possessions when divided by the total number of applicants studied amounts to but $23.84 per person. These striking disclosures in the face of a per capita wealth in Pennsylvania in 1922 of $1,754.85 for every man, woman and child, undoubtedly, also explain why only about 400 of these aged persons carried any insurance· the great majority paying premiums of less than $12 a year which was generally for fire insurance. In view of this prodigious poverty, one· can hardly, in fairness, accuse these people of any lack of inclination to be thrifty. Obviously, any savings would be impossible of accomplishment under the existing conditions. Of all other sources of income, 11 applicants had some income from investments, seventeen from properties, two from small businesses, 32 from lodgers and roomers, six were receiving pensions from the government, 17 from industrial corporations while 22 applicants were helped by fraternal orders, 2 by trade unions and one was in the receipt of a state teacher's pension.

What the Aged Need.

The moderate demands of these aged are pathetic indeed. The overwhelming majority of the applicants having, at best, lived a hand-to-mouth existence, their present wants are indeed frugal. Many of them state they could find sufficient comfort if the State were to give them a sum even below the maximum allowed by law. Their necessities of life are only those things which are indispensable to human existence. They have lived a lifetime on pitifully small wages and have developed a most provident method of existence; and do not ask for more from the Commonwealth in the promotion of whose welfare their lives were spent. Of the nearly 1,000 persons who accounted for their expenditures on food· 9 out of every 10 applicants declared that these items amount to less than $10 per week, while 6 out of every 10 of these aged get along on less than $5.00 per week for food. The larger expenditures are given only by married couples. Two-thirds of these applicants spend less than $10 a month for their rent, and only in the case of the larger centers and married couples do the rentals paid by these applicants amount to $15 a month and over. This would seem good evidence that

that of the extra expenditures required by the aged the.1
items given -were for medicines and taxes, the latter of
especially burdensome to those who had little homes
course, many needed some extra money for clothes, repa
homes, or feed for their chickens or cows which they pos
the case of a number of applicants, church and lodge d
as mortgage payments were very important items of reg
ditures. There were a number of cases who, like the w
a western county who at 74 supported an invalid sist€
needed some extra help because they were helping, as best
some other dependents.

Characters of Applicants as Commented Upon by th€
Employers

Testimony of the good character of the applicants s
secured by our Commission from yet another source. A ‹
letter of inquiry was addressed to a randomly selected li
350 former employes of these applicants. The letter inqui
ing the "character, industry, stability and general reput€
applicant both as employe and citizen." Of the letters ;
were returned "undelivered," 27 applicants could not be i‹
their former employers, while definite replies were rec
238 concerns. Of this total, only eight commented ac
garding the reputation of the applicants either as empl‹
citizens. The rest all received "good" or "excellent"
tions. Most of these men, and even many women, ha‹
ployed by these concerns for many years. The 238 cor
worked for a period of 2,585 years making an average ‹
of service with one employer to whom they rendered ex
vice. And many employers, aware of the plight of these
pressed the hope that the State will, at least, be able
these worthy and deserving producers. Some of the cc

Pennsylvania and he ought to have all the assistance he can get. He is a man about 70 years and seems to have no near relatives of any kind.

"This woman (testifies the Board of Education of a third class city) is the oldest living teacher in this county, respected by all. Very feeble, of sound mind and best of character, unable to do anything and no support. She served faithfully for years', started when very young and left out owing to her age and will likely be a charge unless some way can be found to support her. By taking the matter up with any of our oldest and best citizens they will vouch for the above.

"The above named," writes a colleries' concern, "will be eighty-four years of age this coming February. He is an Austrian by birth; has been in this country over fifty years and has worked for this company for a period of over thirty years as a timberman. His character is unquestionable, perfectly honest, and was a very industrious man during his working period He is very much thought of wherever I have investigated in the several communities visited where at one time or other he had lived."

The superintendent of a well known railroad company writing about an applicant states:—"I consider his character, industry, stability and general reputation of the highest both as an employee and citizen and consider him worthy of any assistance which the above commission may see fit to give him."

Other abbreviated comments follow:

"Old type mechanic—changing styles incapacitated him."

"Was one of old time faithful employes. Wish we had more of his type now."

"If he asked for aid, it is because he is no longer able to earn a living."

"After eighteen years of service, I have only words of praise concerning him."

"At the end of life's journey and certainly deserves assistance."

"On account of his age and health we could no longer use him."

"If I were able, I would personally help him."

"On the job every day for 20 years—even against the advice of his physician."

"Considerably above the average in stability, loyalty and general reputation."

"Character above reproach."

"Widow employed in bank for twelve years. Was quite industrious and capable, but had to quit on account of old age and sickness."

"He worked for us just as long as he was able and his character, industry, stability and general reputation are all of the best."

"Miner from 1876 until 1920, at which time it was necessary to cease on account of old age and miners' asthma."

"Worked days when it was not fit for a man of his age to be out. Nevertheless he stayed with us through rough and good. When plant was closed, he was laid off."

"Mr. O. was in our employ from September 1906 to March 1920. His duties were that of night watchman; while in our employ he was a very faithful, concientious employe. He was obliged to give up his work owing to not being physically able to perform the labors any longer. The writer has known Mr. O. personally for twenty-one years and has known him to be a man of excellent character and industrious insofar as his health would permit, and a good citizen in every way. He owns a small house in which he and his daughter live together. The daughter has been an invalid for over twenty years and is able only to get around the house and do little things for her father. Mr. O. is now confined to his bed most of the time. His son, who is in our employ, tries to get his father up each night for a little while. I do not know that he has any income of any kind and think his main support is what his son can give him. The writer believes that Mr. O. is worthy of your consideration and assistance."

"I have throughly investigated the general reputation of this man covering the past twenty or more years and find that he worked for the above company for about ten years until he became too old and was stricken with miners' asthma and since that time has been practically kept by neighbors' charity, a small weekly allowance from the Knights of Pythias and was furnished free coal and frequent help from this company. His wife died a short time ago and he is now without any home of his own but is being taken care of for the present I believe by a son who, however, has a large family himself and is hard pressed to see that they get along. I believe that he is very worthy of any help you may be able to give him."

"Mr. C. was employed by me for five years as fireman at my saw-mill but now, owing to his age and health, he has not been able to do a days' work for almost a year. The last work he did for me he was not in condition to do as I later found him lying on his face and it was apparent that he had fainted. He was very prompt and reliable all the time he worked for me. His reputation is very good. He was a very peaceable, law abiding citizen. He is very badly in need of help as winter is coming on and they have nothing to go on with. I know they will appreciate any help you can give them."

"Regarded him as one of our most faithful employes."

"Very industrious worker for twenty-two years. Poor health now."

"Industrious worker for thirty years. Excellent character."

"I take pleasure in stating that the character, industry, stability and reputation is irreprochable both as a citizen and employe."

"On account of bad eyesight and feebleness left our employ. Sorry to lose him, but he could not continue his work."

"Handicapped by physical conditions."

"Too old to work—Sunday school and church worker. No bad habits."

"A man to be depended upon—needs help badly."

"Burdened with family troubles which consumed what little he managed to save."

"Laid off after eighteen years of service on account of rheumatism. Could no longer work."

"Very satisfactory worker for twenty-five years. Was a very powerful man physically, but is now a walking skeleton as a result of sickness."

"Honest, law-abiding citizen worthy of assistance. An old man of sterling integrity and if he has applied for assistance, I am certain he needs it."

"Forty years of steady, sober, hard-working and faithful employment. Good citizen."

"A privilege to testify for so worthy a subject, who is much in need of help."

"Always used his earnings to help other people and is now left without sufficient funds. All caused through self-sacrifice."

"Sixteen years of faithful work. Old age against him."

"Railroad watchman relieved from service; over age limit."

"This man worked too hard, night and day, until old age made him cease."

"Thirty years of steady, reliable work."

"Twenty years work—excellent reputation, fine gentleman."

"Thirteen years of service. Glad of the opportunity to say something in favor of this man."

"Record of thirty years, excellent."

"Forty-two years of honorable and upright service."

"Clear record where he was employed from August 29, 1869 until April 1, 1921."

The following are the most striking of the few of the adverse comments made:

"He is a right good old fellow in many ways, but drinks anything he can get hold of and doesn't try to work as steadily as he could, nor to conserve his earnings as he should. He is not a bad fellow but just a little trifling."

"Twenty-four years of service; while in our employ was quite a heavy drinker. We know, however, that during the late years he has discontinued drinking."

"A man that don't look ahead when he has money, but is a peaceful citizen and a good neighbor."

"He is not worn out from work, but perhaps from the excessive use of tobacco."

Summary

Thus, the foregoing analysis of the actual conditions and char ter of the aged applicants in the State shows conclusively that modern problem of dependency in old age is not necessarily t of individual maladjustment, not the result of any lack of ind try, or the inclination to be thrifty, but is due largely to our v industrial expansion which, increasingly, finds less and less rc for the decrepit aged worker or farmer. With the advantages mechanical experiences decreasing continuously as machines steadily replacing human skill; and frequently, after a lifeti of toil at a mere subsistence wage, finding themselves with friends and relatives able to help, the declining days of the aged n and woman are, indeed, bleak and despairing. For, even more p ful than poverty and suffering in youth, is that of old age wl "hope no longer springs eternal in the human breast." To the n and woman past seventy years of age, the morrow can, by stretch of imagination, be made to seem brighter than yesterday

As we studied them, the aged dependents seem to fall into following groups:

(a) the industrial class who work for low wages all their liv live a hand to mouth existence and who, when physically wor out, have been dropped from the rolls by their employers with any means;

The following two cases illustrate the point at issue:

(b) the poor farmer, especially the farm laborer, who at best never obtained more than a bare subsistence and who, when old, has nothing to fall back upon;

(c) the widow who has always depended for support upon her husband, but who is left without support upon his death;

(d) the unmarried person who never earned much, or whose savings vanished somehow and who has no one to turn to—this being true of even some professional people; and

(e) the large group of persons from all classes against whom fate has turned and who have lost their accumulated means of support either through sickness, poor investments, accidents, and the like. A great many people in this class are found to be really above the

> The story of R. S. illustrates the difficulties facing the ambitious working man :— Born in the state with practically no schooling whatsoever, he started picking slate at the age of nine. He then worked for a railroad company for about thirty-nine years as a machinist and during twenty-five years did not lose one weeks work. He averaged a good wage and was never disciplined. Even at the age of sixty-three, he went to the Panama Canal because he heard "they pay higher wages there". He stayed there three years. Despite his raising eleven children and sending two girls through high school, he managed to save up a good deal of money and invested $2,500 with a brokerage company in New York which failed; bought $1,200 worth of railroad stock and invested $1,000 in rubber stock, both of which are worthless, and still claims $1,000 invested in oil stocks, which he hopes will "come out all right some day."

average in kindness towards others; and the "improvidence" of many of these consist chiefly in their being endowed with a greater measure of generosity, self-sacrifice, and trust in human beings than is the case of the more successful of us. The complexities of our present civilization are beyond the simple and trusty souls of some of these "old fashioned" folks and the people in whom they place their confidence frequently do not live up to their expectations.*

---

*Mr. C. B. has finally learned a lesson that generosity does not pay in this harsh world, although he can profit little by this. This man, who is now existing upon practically nothing and at the same time is trying to take care of an invalid daughter, was once a wealthy merchant and was known throughout the district for his generosity. He endorsed the notes of all who came to him. As a result he lost over $20,000 and he sold his merchandise store to pay for some of the notes.

The poem below which needs no comment, was written by a talente woman about an old physician whose application is now in the hand of his local board:—

"A TRIBUTE TO AN OLD FRIEND.

I traveled back to the old-home town,
Though none of my own yet stay;
I walked again in the paths I trod
So oft in a by-gone day.

The loneliest place in the world
Were the streets of the old-home town.
For scarce a familiar face I saw
As I wandered up and down.

For some are asleep on the western hill,
And many are gone away,
And those that remain are greatly changed.
For all toll to time must pay.

But one I knew I should find the same
Though touched by the years that fly,
As these maples throw a wider shade
And their arms reach wondrous high.

I sought him out in his lonely home,
My father's old friend and mine,
And looked into eyes that, dimmed by age,
With deep human kindness shine.

For this man was not my friend alone;
He has served through many years,
Where'er were need or sorrow or pain,
Wherever flowed human tears.

A doctor he of an olden school,
With heart open wide to all,
Who answered with equal care and speed
The rich and the poor man's call.

And oft far out on the lonely road—
No car made his labor light—
He drove alone through Summer's heat,
Winter's cold or day or night.

And many bills yet remain unpaid,
For he would not oppress the poor,
But a bounteous treasure he has earned
Awaits on that shining shore.

May he live and die in the old-home town,
Still loved and revered by all,
And enter a mansion all his own
When he answers the last sweet call."

Obviously, the facts cited above, warrant a revaluation of our attitude toward these dependent aged. The problems facing the old, being effects of our present complex civilization, can no longer be solved by each individual. Being definitely a result of our present maladjusted social structure, the remedy to be prescribed must, therefore, be quite different from the one inaugurated three centuries ago and which we still follow ardently. In every phase of industrial and economic endeavor we have had the courage to break with all the impediments of the obsolete past; have we not then also the courage to break with some of our obviously outworn and degrading social anachronisms?

CHAPTER V.

ESTIMATED COST OF OLD AGE ASSISTANCE IN PENNSYLVANIA

Not infrequently, even the friends of old age assistance legislation, who are fully aware of the justices and humanity of this new method of caring for our dependent aged and are conscious of its sore need, point to the numerous new activities undertaken by our government and contend that the State is assuming too many burdens; and that the cost of this plan, even conceding its worthiness and merit, is beyond the present ability of the State; that the taxpayer is already overloaded and that this is not the time to add to his encumbrances. This is all due to a generally accepted, though erroneous, impression that any consideration of an old age assistance plan would be financially prohibitive. The court complainants against the Act went even further, and with a total disregard for facts, contended, in their brief and in their agitation throughout the State, that "the minimum cost of the old age pension system, if enforced in accordance with the provisions of the Act of Assembly will be approximately $25,000,000 per annum for the next ten years". Without any facts to support them, they based their estimate upon an imaginary assumption that one-third of the persons seventy years of age and over in the State, would qualify for assistance under the Act.

Old Age Assistance Feasible and Economical

Now, at this juncture, we are not concerned, of course, with the ethical question as to what should be considered first — human values, or monetary considerations. Nor shall we dwell on the doubtful wisdom or possibility of economizing in our relationship with the socially dependent classes. We have had sufficient warnings that frequently what seems a temporary economy, along these lines, is an exceedingly expensive program in the long run. We shall leave these considerations for the reader to decide. At this time, we shall confine ourselves to a presentation of simple facts, confident that these will show that an effective old age assistance plan in Pennsylvania would not only impose no considerable burdens upon the taxpayers, but that it is a most feasible and economical method of care of the dependent aged. The figures cited below will, we hope, prove conclusively that neither the number of persons suggested by the complainants as qualifying under the Pennsylvania law, nor the total, estimated by them as the amount this would cost the State, have any bases in fact whatsoever. The utter absurdity of these contentions are obvious from the following:

According to the United States census of 1920, the population of Pennsylvania that year was 8,720,017. The same census shows that of this total 226,933, or 2.6 for every hundred population, were persons 70 years of age and over; in other words, for every 1,000 persons in the State, 26 are 70 years of age and over. Now, if the arguments of the opposition should be correct, at least 8.7 of every 1,000 persons in the state would qualify for old age assistance under our law. This would mean that, at least a total of 75,644 persons would qualify for assistance. How little foundation there is for this, is evident below.

TABLE NO. XIII. OLD AGE ASSISTANCE AND OVERHEAD COSTS

County	Total Number of Applications Received	Number Approved	Number Rejected	Average Allowance Per Year Per Applicant	Total Spent by County Board on Overhead	Cost of Overhead Per Applicant
Adams	80	39	15	$277 44	$92 37	$1 71
Beaver	114	55	53	264 00	114 00	1 00
Bedford	132	97	5	120 00	154 64	1 51
Berks	133	50		240 00	15.70	.31
Bradford	243	128	20	147 00	35.77	24
Butler	17	1		336.00	[1]	[1]
Cameron	29	16	13	135 00	14 31	49
Centre	175	155	5	180 00	97 47	60
Chester	56	40	6	219 36	113 83	2 47
Clarion	15				[2]	[2]
Clinton	100	50	50		[1]	[1]
Columbia	43	37	1	360 00	[2]	[2]
Crawford	112	84	2	242 28	[2]	[2]
Erie	79	3	28		88 32	2 84
Fulton	35	31	4	162 96	199 00	5 65
Huntingdon	110	82	20	104 40	253 93	2 48
Indiana	123	70	9	300 00	90 00	1 13
Jefferson	173	131	29	355 80	100 00	62
Lycoming	98	87	11	292 32	125 80	1 28
McKean	94	80	14	286 44	38 00	40
Mercer	241	45	10	231 60	33 88	61
Mifflin	47	45	2	276 00	[1]	[1]
Monroe	14	11	3	360 00	[2]	[2]
Montour	27	12	4	328 92	[1]	[1]
Northumberland	133	86	2	243 00	119 25	1 34
Pike	14	7		360 00	10 80	1 54
Potter	34				[2]	[2]
Somerset	156	102	9	242 52	89 32	80
Sullivan	10	5		336 00	15.70	3 14
Susquehanna	71				[2]	[2]
Tioga	150	68	12	192 00	72 30	90
Union	66	66		205 44	[2]	[2]
Venango	107	15	3	216 00	[2]	[2]
Warren	70	29			10 75	37
Washington	70	50	6		12 70	22
Westmoreland	170	19		196 80	[1]	[1]
Total	3,341	1,796	336	$248 66	$1,897 84	$1 04

Probable Cost

In preparation for this report, we have been able to study the findings of thirty-six counties whose total population amounts to 2,393,001, or, approximately 27.4 per cent of the population in the State. These counties are also representative of all sections of the State. Practically all our local old age assistance boards in these counties have been very active since their organization. They have been in existence on the average more than eight months each; and have been receiving applications steadily since the day of their organization. Most of them have done a good deal of scouring through their respective counties and, by means of extensive publicity, urged all qualified persons; despite the meager appropriations available, to file their applications with their respective boards. By November, the thirty-six local boards received a total of 3,341 applications. Estimates made by these boards as to the approximate percentage the applications already received represent the total possible number in the respective counties show that while a number of county boards think that they already have more than three-fourths of the

[1] None.
[2] Not given.

applications in, some believe that the applications already filed with them constitute barely one-third or less of the possible total which may apply when the act becomes fully operative. Considering these estimates together, however, it appears that the applications received up to November represent at least 57.2 of the entire possible total. The total applications already filed with the various boards indicate that the number of applicants who have already applied are to the ratio of 1.9 per 1,000 population in these counties. This means that when this is increased 42.8 per cent, the total probable ratio of applicants would not exceed 3.3 per thousand. Assuming that this ratio should hold true for the entire State, it would mean that the total number of applicants in Pennsylvania would not exceed 28,776. At an average allowance of $248.66 per year, as found to be the average for 29 counties—although the maximum average of $360 per applicant given in four counties would obviously be somewhat reduced after the State Commission had gone over these recommendations—it would mean an expenditure of $7,155,440.16 per year.

Actual Cost

But, it must be remembered that this is based upon the total number of applications filed with the county boards. As a matter of fact, of the 2,132 applications upon which these boards have been able up to November, to decide definitely, we find that 336 or 15.8 per cent of these were rejected entirely. Assuming that, at least this percentage would hold true throughout the State when money becomes available—and the likelihood of rejections will obviously be greater then—and giving no consideration to the fact that probably a considerable percentage would be disapproved by the State Commission, which has a final check-up on these—it would mean that there could not possibly be more than 24,230 grants made, involving a total of $6,025,031.89 per year, or an expenditure of sixty-nine cents for each citizen of the State and sixty-seven cents per $1,000 taxable property and 35 cents per $1,000 wealth of the State.

Now, if we should spend the sum of $6,025,031.80 per year, we would be able to take care of more than three times the number of people now supported in our almshouses, upon which institutions we are now making an annual cash expenditure of approximately $6,000

*Estimates regarding the present expenditures on poor relief made by our various county and local poor districts show that:

In the ten year period—1914—1923—our sixty-seven counties raised $95,000,000 for poor relief purposes. In 1922—the last year for which complete figures are available—our counties spent approximately $5,550,000 on the maintenance of their almshouses: they gave more than $1,500,000 in outdoor relief; and with a number of smaller items the aggregate expenditures for poor purposes were well nigh $10,000,000.

The most important instruments through which we are caring for our indigent poor are our 85 almshouses or poor farms varying in size to accommodate from 1 to over 1,000; exhibiting wide differences in equipment and administration. These almshouses report a value of land, building and equipment of over $16,000,000 and own over 17,000 acres of land of which more than 10,000 were reported to be under cultivation.

To support an average of more than 8,000 poor in our almshouses in 1922, we spent over $2,000,000 on their direct maintenance and expended almost $3,500,000 on our almshouse overhead. It took over 1,000 paid employees to look after the inmates of our almshouses.

'000.* And this item does not include the thousands of dollar of food consumed in the county homes, which is raised on the farms; nor does this total include the interest on the over $ 000 investment involved in these county homes, only five per

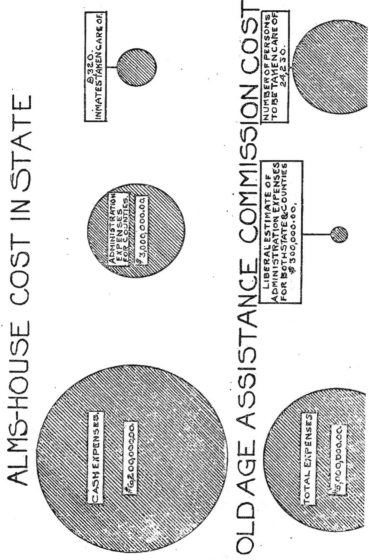

which would add $800,000 more to the total cost, thus makin expenditure of, at least, $7,000,000 per year on less than o the number of persons we could support in their own hon much happier fashion and without the odious stigma of pau Again, when it is remembered that a study of the possession applicants shows that approximately 17.3 per cent of the total amount of the pensions granted would revert back to the State through the properties of the applicants, which are to be taken over by the State under the law, and from which proceeds, after the death of the applicant, the full amount paid by the State is collected with interest, THE ACTUAL TOTAL COST PER YEAR WOULD REALLY NOT EXCEED $5,000,000, OR 57 CENTS PER CAPITA. Is there a citizen in this Commonwealth who would not rather be willing to pay this fifty-seven cents, or fifty-six cents per $1,000 taxable property and only twenty-four cents per $1,000 wealth of the State—even if these were additional, which happily is not the case— than be responsible for the tragedies and heart-breaks now caused by the prospect of the poorhouse after a lifetime of toil and service?

Furthermore, of the approximately $5,500,000 cash spent on our almshouses in the year 1922, nearly $3,500,000, or more than 60 per cent of the total were spent on the administration of the system; only $2,000,000 going directly to the inmates. Even under liberal estimates, our Commission is convinced from present studies of the facts that even if we had a fund of $5,000,000 a year the administrative expenses, for both state and counties, would not exceed $300,000 per year. As seen from the preceding table, the cost for investigation per applicant in the 26 counties from which county treasurers' figures were obtained shows that the average cost per applicant amounts to $1.04 ,or less than forty-one cents per $100 allowed. Three-fourths of these applications, according to the statement of these local boards, would not have to be re-investigated when money becomes available. In the budget submitted by our Commission, we are only asking for $15,000 administrative expenses for each million dollar appropriation, for which sum we feel we could adequately handle the situation. In view of all this, can there still be doubt as to the incomparable cheapness and efficiency of the present law? And can the complainants still scoff at the "maudlin sentimentality" of the advocates of this legislation?

CHAPTER VI.

CONSTITUTIONALITY OF OLD AGE ASSISTANCE ACT QUESTIONED

As already pointed out before, hardly did the Commission manage to complete its organization when a Bill of Complaint was filed praying for an injunction to restrain the State Commission and the fiscal officers of the State from "making disbursements involving the Commonwealth of Pennsylvania in great expense to the irreparable injury of ourselves and other taxpayers."

The complainants argued that in addition to violating Section 1 of Article III of the Pennsylvania Constitution which provides tha "No appropriations, except for pensions or gratuities for militai services, shall be made for charitable, educational or benevolent pu poses, to any person or community nor to any denominational ; sectarian institution, corporation or Association," the law grants tl Commission arbitrary powers in making grants and is, therefore, a improper delegation of legislative power; that it is discriminatoi in its age limit and other qualifications, and therefore violates tl Fourteenth Amendment of the Constitution of the United Stat which prohibits any State from denying to any person within i jurisdiction the equal protection of the law; that the Act violat the Constitution in granting special privileges and that it is appr priating public money for a private purpose.

At the hearing before the Dauphin County judges, and in h extensive brief, the attorney for the complainants attacked the la as "bordering on a new form of outrageous socialism;" characte ized it as "grotesque, full of absurdities, and a 'jig-saw' puzzle," ai argued that this Act is a "distinct step toward centralization ai toward making thriftlessness and laziness genteel." It is tl menacing spectre of the poorhouse over the hill, declared the attorn for the complainants, that is responsible for our efforts and ambitio Remove that dreaded apparition, and what becomes of our civi zation?

The State's Attorney General through Deputy Attorney Gener Philip S. Moyer, in defending the Act, argued that the constitution restrictions regarding benevolent appropriations, as shown concl sively throughout the debates at the Constitutional Convention, we not intended for the purposes contended by the complainants b were inserted for the purpose of preventing the steady flow of calaï ity bills which were prevalent at that period. The State, Mr. Moy pointed out, has repeatedly appropriated money to certain defini classes of dependents. As to the wisdom and merits of the law, t State expostulated that it is not for the court to pass upon, the latt being solely the prerogative of the legislative branch.

On August 4, 1924, the Dauphin County court rendered a decisi.

'The question before us is whether the old age assistance provided by this statute involves an appropriation for charitable or benevolent purposes and whether the prohibition "to any person" includes a prohibition to a class of persons through the agency of a commission."

After finding the act allowing "benevolences to a person," the court states further:

"The money for this purpose is appropriated by the Commonwealth. This certainly is a kindness towards persons in old age. This Act manifests a desire to do good; it indicates a love toward mankind; an effort to promote happiness; in fact, it comes within all of the definitions of benevolence. The appropriations must, therefore, be characterized as one for a 'benevolent purpose.' Is it not within the class of appropriations for 'benevolent purposes' which Section 18 of Article III of the Constitution prohibits? The prohibition is against any appropriation for charitable, educational or benevolent purposes to any person or community * * *

"If we are right in our conclusions that the prohibition for benevolence to any person is as broad as the language plainly indicates, then we say there is not a syllable in the Constitution which authorized a system of benevolence through a State Department or agency, for the care and maintenance of aged indigent residents of the State. This argument is tantamount to saying that the Legislature can pass a law to do the thing indirectly which the Constitution prohibits it from doing directly. If appropriations can be made to a Commission the purpose of which is to distribute benevolence to aged indigent persons, it is accomplishing exactly what the Constitution says cannot be done, namely, making an appropriation for benevolent purposes to certain persons. * * *"

"Pennsylvania has recognized its inherent duty to care for its poor. Its system had been in operation many years when the Constitution of 1874 was framed. That system provided for poor districts, poor directors and overseers, and for the relief of paupers as a matter of local concern. Those who framed the Constitution understood it, and no word is contained in the Constitution with reference to it. The system was left untouched. If there had been any purpose to change that system, some word indicating that purpose would have been found in the Constitution. If it had been intended that direct appropriations might be made out of the State Treasury for the relief of the poor, some provision evidencing such intention, which would create so radical a change in the governmental policy in this regard, would have been inserted in the Constitution. The conclusion is, therefore, irresistible that a direct appropriation from the State Treasury to any person

or class of persons, cannot be sustained on the theor
that it is a discharge of the inherent obligation of th
State to take care of its paupers. * * *"

An appeal, from this decision, was promptly taken to tl
Supreme Court and a hearing was held in Philadelphia bef
body on November 28th. Further briefs were submitted by
Attorney General Moyer and special deputy Robert J. Ste
Philadelphia. In their briefs the State's attorneys again
out that the prohibitive clause in Section 18 of Article II]
biguous because if it was intended to give it the meaning cc
by the Dauphin County Court there was no necessity for t
tional clause "to any person or community." The insertion
latter was obviously for the purpose of prohibiting approp
only to individuals, as is clearly brought out in the Debate
Constitutional Convention. Furthermore, the briefs pointed
if the Dauphin County Court decision should be sustained thi
jeopardize not only the Mothers' Assistance Act, but could
construed as prohibiting every State retirement provision as
of "benevolence." For, if the Constitution permits only gr
for "military services", it is obvious that it precludes any of
vices. It would seem, therefore, that no interpretation could
that, under this limitation, retirement gratuities could be]
State services whereby the state pays in full or in part pens
a time when no services are being rendered. Retirement pr
under these conditions would obviously be "benevolent" all(
The argument that this is merely compensation for previoi
services rendered, could hardly be upheld in view of this int
tion that no service can be compensated except "military
If so, neither the judges', teachers', nor state employees' re
systems can be proved valid.

Again, it is also clear that, if, as the court declares, the leg
can not do anything indirectly which the constitution pro.
from doing directly, it would be difficult to sustain state ap
tions to charitable institutions or hospitals. For when Johi
a poor man, spends fourteen days in a hospital free of cha
the State, under the present system of appropriations, reco
the hospital, through the State Department of Welfare, for 1
ber of free days service rendered at, let us say, $3.00 per da
this a direct appropriation of $42.00 benevolence to Joh
through the hospital?

The fundamental philosophy of the complainants in se(
understanding of the reasons which motivated them to att

"What," queries the attorney for the complainants, "is the necessity of declaring our system of poor relief inadequate?....We are told that 'ideas as to social responsibility change in fifty years'. It is difficult to see how a change 'in the whole course of industry', or even the invention of railroads, radios and aeroplanes, has changed the nature of pauperism,.....while 'ideas as to social responsibility change in fifty years,' the construction of our Constitution does not change. SOCIAL AND ECONOMIC CONSIDERATIONS HAVE NO PLACE IN ITS INTERPRETATION."

"The system of pensions to the aged is a novelty in this country. It furnishes a brand new 'sluice-way' for carrying away the money of the taxpayers. It is true that the system has obtained some footing in other countries....In the House of Commons, this summer just passed, there was an extended discussion as to relaxing the requirements of Old Age Pensions. Sentimental arguments were made against any age limit, and against any inquiry as to outside means; the dear old folks did not like to tell their ages or what their savings were. This was reminiscent of the Pennsylvania legislator who did not care whether the Pennsylvania treasury went broke; his mission was to prevent hearts being broken." (We shall leave it to the reader to decide upon the respective merits of treasuries and hearts.)

"Everyone sympathizes with the poor, and especially the aged poor. Many sympathize practically by charitable work and contributions. Others, like jurymen and legislators, are willing to vote the money of other people in order to relieve their own sympathies. Two points of practical wisdom should not be overlooked: (1) to the extent to which the State affects to afford universal panaceas for the ills and shortcomings of human nature and human institutions, private charity, that gentle dew from heaven, will dry at the source; (2) the stigma of the poorhouse, so movingly deplored by appellants, is a salutary economic factor; THE REASONABLE DREAD AND APPREHENSION OF "OVER THE HILL TO THE POORHOUSE" MAY BE A NEEDED STIMULUS TO A SELF-RESPECTING, THRIFTY LIFE....THE PRESENT POOR SYSTEM OF THE STATE IS ADMITTEDLY ADEQUATE TO CARE FOR ALL THE POOR OF THE STATE, YOUNG AND OLD." In view of all our preceding discourses, it is hardly necessary to comment upon this Sixteenth Century mind.

It is but natural that in undertaking such novel :
vided by the Old Age Assistance Act there shoul
givings on the part of even those sincerely interes
the present chaotic and humiliating conditions. V
arguments brought against old age assistance l
ludicrous and far-fetched as to hardly warrant a
there are some, we felt, that merited some furth
Frequently, even proponents of this measure expres:
inauguration of this system of caring for the aged i1
would perhaps "strike a blow at the incentive for 1
"reward the shiftless and unworthy." It is also fea
an effective old age assistance system would "rem(
support from children who are able but unwilling
parents"; and "would cause reckless spending of
beneficiaries."

Of course, the reader who has perused the prece
ready found the answer to these apprehensions.
many thousands of our aged become utterly depend
the centuries long dread and stigma of the poor-h
sufficient to indicate that the causes of dependency :
to more fundamental causes than individual shiftles
mendations of the employers in regard to these
have shown conclusively how industrious and hon
aged were throughout their lives. It is evide:
few men or women who have habitually led abnor
dent lives manage to survive three-score and ten

able to present but few of these comments. However, of the nearly one-hundred replies only three were inclined to recognize the apprehensions of the opponents. In this connection it is significant to note that these three are members of county boards which have not met since their organization, and as far as we know, have had little or no contacts with aged applicants. The sharpest disagreements with the opposing contentions came from the most active boards. Some of these comments follow:

> "From the experience I have had as investigator of Centre County, I find few arguments not in favor of the Old Age Assistance Act and very few who think it would cause reckless spending. Ninety per cent of our people who have made application certainly are worthy of assistance.
>
> Take the J. R. family—father 74—mother 70—idiotic 'baby' 38 years old. The 'baby' has always been perfectly helpless; the mother crippled by having a broken hip that was never taken care of because they did not have the money; father has the worst form of cancer of legs and not able to earn anything but just depending on the help their daughter gives them, and her husband is just a laborer, with a family of children. They are absolutely destitute and it certainly did not come from fast living. This is one case out of 155 which we know what a little help could do. It would be a blessing instead of creating 'reckless spending'."
>
> Rebecca C. Tuten, Secretary,
> Centre County Board."

> "The applicants we have received so far are good, worthy Christians and have called on us for assistance because they are in need and dislike to ask for aid from their townships because of the indignity attached to such a request. In several cases my applicants will have to submit to aid from their townships very shortly.
>
> All applicants that I have received have been men who received about a dollar a day before the war and have little education and no trade, and have often raised large families. On account of their small wages and heavy expenses they have been unable to protect themselves against their old age. Neither are their children who are also poor, able to adequately support themselves and their children and their old fathers. None of my applicants have been shiftless or unworthy. Where any applied who had children or near relatives who are able to support them, no consideration was given the application.
>
> Shem Spigelmyer,
> Lycoming County Board."

> "We have had ninety-four applications that we have passed upon. We reported eighty favorably and refused

fourteen; principally because there were fairly well-to-do children who ought to care for the old people.

Of those whom we recommended from Bradford, our largest city in the county, there were only four who may have been drinking men. Possibly some others were shiftless in their younger days, but some way the majority of those whom we met and visited and inquired about seemed self-respecting people who, for various reasons, seemed unable to get ahead. There were very few cases when the children, however poor, were not willing to help their parents.

Mae E. Choate, Chairman,
McKean County Board."

"Having had twenty-seven years of experience with old people in granting charity to them, the Old Age Assistance law is the only superb act of a State to relieve suffering among our worthy poor. Hoping our law-makers will see it in that light.

Edwin S. Crone, Secretary
York County Board."

"There is no foundation for the statements mentioned above in regard to the Old Age Assistance Act in my opinion. Have been in business in Emporium for more than forty years and I am well satisfied that the Act, if put in operation, will greatly benefit several worthy, industrious, sober men, who have been unfortunate in accumulating a competency.

L. K. Huntingdon,
Cameron County Board."

"It is possible that some who suffer in old age have have been shiftless and ignorant, but we cannot for such reasons escape the responsibility to help them when old age brings poverty and want. If the State does not help them the County must and if the County fails, it falls upon the individual citizen.

It is a bitter pill for parents to force unwilling children to support them. I find very very few cases where such unwillingness exists. A large number of our applicants never have been able to earn enough to live comfortably and their children are like them. This is the curse of the common laborer.

Whether the allowance is spent wastefully depends largely upon the carefulness of the County Board. The amount granted should make reckless spending impossible. Persons over seventy years of age are entirely unlikely to be spend-thrifts.

Rev. John T. Judd, Chairman,
Union County."

"I have found but two or three shiftless or unworthy out of my one hundred and thirty applicants. For the most part my old folks have simply been unfortunate. Many of them making one dollar a day or much less; sickness and death came and then if they had scraped a little together for their old age—along came the War. After that the very high cost of living, excessive rents and very soon their savings and earnings would go. You know, we are not all financiers.

I do not think the unworthy or shiftless apply for Old Age Assistance. They know investigation would prove them unworthy. I have found that old folks, as a rule, are truthful.

Mrs. Herbert J. Vastine, Secretary,
Berks County Board."

"Our Board has investigated probably one-third of the applications sent in. I feel that in the majority of cases the applicants are not shiftless or unworthy. Of course, as in all movements of this kind, some will creep in, but if the Board is conscientious and does its duty in investigating thoroughly, the burden of supporting the aged will not be shifted from those able to support them on to the State. My experience in investigating has been that it is mostly through inability to work and sickness that aid is asked for and I feel the money would be wisely used.

Mrs. John C. Silsley, Secretary,
Westmoreland County Board."

"If you have worked to your best knowledge and made your living, perhaps helped other less fortunate, and then when you get to be seventy and must secure work, you know what the answer will be—('oh, he is too old'). This, I think, is so cruel. Our country needs to look kindly to our dear fathers and mothers. Maybe they were extravagant but we can give them a little help and there isn't anymore extravagance; and the dear ones will be happy. I am convinced that no one who has ever had an old father or mother will refuse to make them happy in their old days and will help in getting this Act put into effective operation.

Mrs. Janet Workman, Secretary,
Washington County Board."

"The Old Age Board will not grant assistance to the shiftless or unworthy. Every case is thoroughly investigated and only those who are in extreme need are compensated. When children are able to support parents, no help is given. We have found a great many people who have been married but have no relatives.

Mrs. M. H. Swan, Secretary,
Huntingdon County Board."

"The applications sent by this Board have been very carefully investigated and only those sent in that are entirely worthy. Those that are shiftless and not worthy, we negative to your Board. I think the Commission would be a great benefit to the worthy old and poor.

Amos G. Gotwals, Chairman,
Chester County Board."

"In regard to the validity of the above arguments, I will say that in my opinion the opponents of this law are bringing these arguments up for the sake of debating the law, but they do not know such facts to be so. In my experience with the applicants personally and in my experience with the Board work in rejecting those who are not worthy of grant, I find that they are very deserving of such compensation as the law provides.

To my mind, these poor old people who have given the best they had in labor and good citizenship, and many of them raised large families of children, who are now contributing their bit to industry and to their State and Nation, should be as much entitled to a pension as our ex-judges who received enough during their term of office so they should be able to take care of themselves. How do they get around the Constitution to pay such pensions?

Leon C. Baynes, Secretary,
Tioga County Board.".

"The contentions of the opponents could not be possible with careful investigation of applicants and proper precautions. I find in many cases the burden should be removed from their children as it works injury to the children's families and makes the old parents dependent and charitable patients and not pleasant to the ones concerned. In my experience so far, I see a world of good can be done by the law, if not allowed to impose upon it. And oh, to how many cases (especially women) it would prove a wonderful blessing; smooth down their declining years and make their last days, days of pleasure. On fifty cents or one dollar per day for comforts and food they cannot get very extravagant or reckless.

C. R. Hall,
Jefferson County Board."

"All applications passed by our Board are worthy and we consider that the poor aged should receive this State assistance, considering pensions to the various other persons in the State.

A. N. Shearer, Chairman,
Columbia County Board."

"All the above objections are practically without foundation. The applications sent in by the Fulton County Board after due investigation of their merits have been made, have been pronounced worthy as to their claims and the benefit they would receive would give them a more cheerful view of life. I admit that there are a certain few who would try to take advantage and make claims for aid without excuse, but this is a condition that creeps into all benevolent institutions and the number of this class would be negligible. There is no question but that the old people would be better cared for under this system than by any other now in existence. The law should be sustained and I believe it will. The opinion given above is what I have drawn from my experience since being on the Board and feel certain the other two members are of the same opinion.

U. G. Humbert, Secretary,
Fulton County Board."

"I have about eighteen applicants from my district in Clinton County. I think most of them are very worthy. Some would not need a dollar a day and could do with less.

Mrs. Agnes Osner,
Clinton County Board."

"If the Boards of the different counties investigate as thoroughly as the Beaver County Board does, there could be no assistance granted to the 'shiftless and unworthy.' Children who are unwilling to support their parents will, in many cases, do so if the matter becomes known that their parents are applying for aid to the State. The persons who would receive this aid are not the types who would spend recklessly because most of them are accustomed to live carefully and take care of the small amount of money they have. Some of the relatives of these people could take care of them for what they would receive.

Mrs. W. B. Gray, Secretary,
Beaver County Board."

"There is no reason that this law should remove the burden of support from the children if Old Age Assistance Boards do their duty. I believe these arguments would not hold good in any case where affairs were administered conscientiously.

Cora M. Dille, Secretary,
Venango County Board."

"I think the motive back of the law is good but could be abused by the members of the Board. To my mind, it will depend on the kind of a Board each County will be able to get.

Horace H. Bittenbender,
Clarion County Board."

"I believe if each County Board only allows what in their opinion would just keep applicants in reasonable comfort, it would remove some of the prejudice against the Act. I think it is largely unjust criticism and of all the applicants for aid whom I have known for some time I cannot say any one of them would have acted different had they known fifty years ago this law would be passed.

B. C. May, Chairman,
Bedford County Board."

"Generally where children are able they are willing to care for their parents. I have had only a few applications where I felt the children were trying to shift the responsibility of the care of their parents.

Mrs. Stacy F. Dean, Secretary,
Mercer County Board."

"The Monroe County Board has received so few applications that I cannot form a definite opinion upon the future influence of the Act upon the applicants. The control of abuses will depend upon the investigations of the local boards.

Dr. Wm. R. Fisher, Secretary,
Monroe County Board."

"It is my belief that the Old Age Assistance would aid a great many people who have been unfortunate and who are worthy of support. I am in favor of it.

Mrs. Carrie H. Stitt, Secretary,
Indiana County Board."

"I have met but few opponents to this law in Somerset County. After fully understanding the Act, the opponents agree it is a good and necessary law. We have a number of applicants who have nothing and are getting a little County aid so that friends or relatives keep them. Why? Because our County Home is overcrowded now, and we have a large home. And the person has a hard heart if it is not touched when these aged and poor with tears plead with you to help them get assistance so that they need not go to the County Home

"To see the necessity of Old Age Assistance one only needs to belong to a County Board a short time. It is charitable work for us, but I feel this to be a great mission work and to live happy we must live for others. Hope the law stands the test.

H. B. Forney, Secretary,
Somerset County Board."

"If all County Boards use the same care in their investigations as our Board has tried to use, I cannot see where the beneficiaries could be reckless in spending the money received. We feel that where the applicants have raised large families who are either unable or unwilling to support them, that they are most deserving of assistance and more so than those who have raised no children and have not spent their money in that way.

John C. Mather,
Bradford County Board."

"I do not believe the above arguments well founded. I can see no reason why it would not be valid if properly executed.

F. A. Osborn, Secretary,
Susquehanna County Board."

"To the validity of the arguments made. by the op-
nents of the Old Age Assistance Law, I would say
t while it may be true in some cases the percent is so
that it is not worth paying any attention.

Levi Fenstermacher·
Montour County Board."

'With proper investigation and supervision these ob-
tions could be overcome.

Mary M. McClean;
Adams County Board."

"I find it the same in this as in everything else—some
e worthy and in need of the support, while others are
t.

Mrs. Orrill W. Avery, Secretary,
Sullivan County Board."

"To this date we have not examined the twenty-seven
)plications received, but will do so soon. I know of a
w who will have no claim; the majority are very
orthy and need this assistance.

Chas. S. Matten,
Snyder County Board."

"The Old Age Assistance Boards, I believe, would be
)le to take proper care of the first objection. If child-
:n, for some reason, do not willingly care for their
irents, such parents should not be compelled to remain
ith them. One would not become very reckless on one
)llar per day in any event. Old people were brought
p in a different age which looked out for the dollar.

George Rosser, Chairman,
Clearfield County Board."·

"The arguments of the opponents are absolutely with-
it foundation and contrary to the facts, as shown by
ie applicants filing claims before the Lycoming County
ld Age Assistance Board. All applicants in the county

(a) The grant is not of sufficient largeness to admit of reckless spending.

(b) Judging from the character of applicants received by the Lycoming County Board, they have without exception been persons who never were addicted to reckless spending. They have been persons who have reared large families on small wages, whose children have become deceased, or of poor means and themselves have large families which tax them to the limit of support; were men who conducted a small business at a small profit, merely eking out an existence until no longer able to attend to business, or who finally failed because of poor business or dishonesty of their customers to pay debts or who through sickness or death in their families have expended what little they had; no derelicts or unworthy have applied. Full amount specified under the Act were recommended only in extreme cases. Amount recommended by the Lycoming County Board varies from $4.00 per month to $30.00 per month; the average amount being $24.36.

John A. Harries, Secretary,
Lycoming County Board."

"This assistance, if obtained, will prove a great blessing to many who gave their lives to humanity but have not succeeded in saving any money.

Mrs. Anna M. Fisher,
Centre County Board."

"My experience, through personal investigation of applicants, leads me to believe that the majority of our aged citizens who are applying for aid are worthy of it. They are, in most cases, parents whose children are laborers struggling with the present day problem of providing for families and the wonder is how they keep their own children housed, clothed and fed without, in addition, providing their parents with a living.

Mrs. F. R. Burdick,
McKean County Board."

"If the County Boards personally investigate the cases, I do not think there will be any trouble. In some of our cases where the children keep their parents, ten dollars per month would mean much to them. As a rule, these are large families. Where there are no children, an old couple could live on twenty-five dollars per month who would not accept money from the town or county.

I hope the law is sustained as it would do so much good.

Mrs. Mazie Brouse, Chairman,
Centre County Board."

"If the Old Age Assistance Boards keeps within the intention of the Bill as it now stands and fully follows

out the intention of same, there would be practically
none who would not, under present conditions, be receiving assistance from the County. I have canvassed
the County many times (Tioga, as well as several others)
and can truthfully say that from my contact with many
that are receiving County aid, the Old Age Assistance
Act would relieve the County from this burden and at
the same time would keep the many old couples together in their declining years where they are now
separated. Besides, it would be cheaper per person to
help maintain same at home instead of at the County
Almhouse.

J. L. Lattimer,
Tioga County Board."

"I believe there is no argument concerning these applications. Our Board very carefully investigates each
petition and studies the individual, makes inquiry that
only the worthy and respectable are recognized. I already know our Board are wholly in sympathy with the
workings of the Old Age Assistance Commission. I think
the State ought to take just such measures, as to insure
the self-respect of old age. Other states have found it a
rightful provision—why not we? It the people of Pennsylvania are desirous of providing an Old Age Fund why
should they be denied the privilege?

Mrs. Hattie Smith, Secretary,
Cameron County Board."

"Through talking with many people of experience I
feel that the Old Age Assistance is going to fill a real
need. I have yet to find one person that objected to the
Old Age Assistance in any way. People at last feel
that a way has been found by which our old people shall
be taken care of in a humane way.

Mrs. L. F. Lambert, Secretary,
Chester County Board."

"The cases we have handled and approved are worthy
and not one dependent because of thriftlessness. Many
old women are struggling to eke out an existence by
doing such work as they can and depending upon charity
for the rest. In many cases sons-in-law are either unable
or unwilling to assist. Daughters are helpless to force
their husbands to assist. In no case where there are
children did we allow the full amount. Our aim is to
give them just enough. I believe the details of cases
would be convincing proof to the Legislature that this
is one of the most worthy pieces of legislation that has
been enacted to assist the unfortunate aged people who
have to take care of themselves in their old age. I am
opposed to shifting the responsibility for them from the
individual to the State but only can say that my ex-

perience in this has been that this would not be so in the cases handled by our Board.

J. H. Reichert, Chairman,
Berks County Board."

"The shiftless and unworthy we have had with us always and will have to the end of the world and because they are human beings they cannot be left to die like dogs. In one way or other the State is bound to provide for them. How could people of little or no means at all be reckless on one dollar a day? When one had settled with the milk-man, paid the rent, the coalman and bought a few necessary clothes and groceries, do you suppose there would be enough left to keep the ordinary man in cigars or the woman in face-powder and ice-cream?

Let us stop fussing and make the last days of the old people—worthy or unworthy—just a bit easier and so may they pass out without bitterness and want.

Mrs. L. J. Waldo, Secretary,
Bradford County Board."

CHAPTER VIII.

IS PUBLIC OPINION IN PENNSYLVANIA BEHIND OLD AGE ASSISTANCE?

We have been asked repeatedly as to what is the attitude of Pennsylvanians towards our pioneer Old Age Assistance Act. Insofar as the public prints and the utterances of public men help to gage the prevailing attitude of the people, the following summarized comments from the press and officials may shed light upon this question:

The Public Ledger—Philadelphia

"The Old Age Pension is in line with the excellent Mothers' Assistance Fund, which helps keep families together. It is always a malancholy sight to see an aged husband and wife, who have spent perhaps fifty years together, sundered by poverty in the last years of their lives."

The Gazette Times—Pittsburgh

"Slow but sure progress of so-called social legislation is indicated by the enactment this year of old age pension laws by the three states, one of them Pennsylvania. The trend toward more charity, but charity dispensed on a higher plane than that of the past is unmistakable. The passing of the dreaded poorhouse is nearing."

The Record—Philadelphia

"The decision of the Dauphin County Court that the old age pension act passed by the last legislature is unconstitutional may be good law, but it certainly is not in accord with the trend of modern humanitarian legislation. Even England, generally classed as a conservative country, has been paying such pensions for many years, and the practice is nearly universal in Europe."

The Press—Pittsburgh

"A Decision of the Dauphin county court in Pennsylvania, declaring the old age pension law unconstitutional, is in line with a lot of other things in this country which have contributed to a widespread conviction that the principle of equal rights is largely a fiction in the actual administration of government.

"The average citizen is becoming heartily sick of the employment of legal technicalities for the benefit of the powerful. He has been looking in vain for the discovery and enforcement of technicalities in behalf of the welfare of the masses of the people.

"The people of Pennsylvania see the judges of the courts and state, county and city employes being retired on substancial pensions, yet the court promptly hoists a stop-sign against a proposal to provide a pittance pension for the aged who have worked hard in private employment".

The Republican—Scranton

"At the very beginning of old age pension legislation in this state it has been made clear that the only way to put it into effect is through an amendment to the state constitution. That it would be adopted if put up to the people, is confidently believed. The idea is growing in other countries as well as in the United States and is regarded as a humane, as well as a wise measure of government.

"A few can understand why a citizen who has contributed his best to organized society in the flower of his youth and the strength of his manhood should be allowed to pass his declining years in poverty and neglect. The fact that there are so many cases of the kind is a forceful commentary upon existing laws."

The Post—Pittsburgh

"After an existance of about a year during which its operation appeared to be a mystery to possible beneficiaries, the old age pension act of the 1923 Pennsylvania

Legislature is now held unconstitutional by the Dauphin County Court. . . . The tradegy of this, after the hopes that had been aroused in a number of aged persons of worthy character, need not be described. . . .

"Having set out to render such assistance to aged persons, the great state of Pennsylvania will scarcely abandon the project. If the higher court should uphold the lower in the decision that the measure is unconstitutional a further argument will be furnished for constitutional revision. While checks in a constitution against what might be called raids on the treasury are appreciated, a proposition to aid the worthy aged of the state who may be in need is not in that class."

The Evening Ledger—Philadelphia

"It is possibly worth while to remind ourselves that a decision of the Dauphin County Court on the constitutionality of an act of the Legislature is not final. . . . It is not likely that the matter will be allowed to rest here. The point raised is too important. . . . That the Legislature and the Governor, both favor the establishment of an old age pension system is clear."

The Times—Scranton

"The Old Age Pension law passed at the last session of the legislature has been declared unconstitutional by the Dauphin county court, and thus does one of Pennsylvania's all too few progressive measures go by the boards."

The Times—Reading

"In handing down the decision, Judge William M. Hargest carefully avoided any expression of the merits of the act. . . . The question of merit, then, is still open. Ought the state take such measures to insure the self-respect of old age? Other states and nations have found it a rightful provision. If the people of Pennsylvania are also desirous of providing an old age assistance fund, should they be denied the privilege of exercising their sovereignty in the matter? They will be unless the constitution is changed so that their will can be carried out in matters of this sort.

"Once again the constitution of this State has been found inadequate with the newer conditions of things as they have developed since the adoption of the present constitution. Within about a month, two measures of popular demand and support, have been killed by antiquated constitutional provisions. First it was the bonus. Now it is the old age assistance fund."

The Times—Erie

"The decision of the Dauphin court is another argument in favor of a constitutional convention. The legislature represented the sentiment of the people when it decided that it would be more humane to pay a small pension to aged persons without means than to send them to the poorhouses, and in all probability the actual cost to the taxpayers would be less. The legislature ought to have the power to give effect to that sentiment in an act of assembly."

The Record—Wilkes—Barre

"...Yet there is much to be said in favor of a systematic plan to give aged dependants some solace in the years of physical and mental inefficiency, rather than have them cast upon the mercy of unwilling relatives or consigning them to the poorhouse. There is nothing more pitiful than the person who is no longer wanted by his employers and is cast aside as a derelict. Whether the advantages are more weighty than the disadvantages is a question to be answered more from experience than from theory."

The Scrantonian—Scranton

"That the old age pension scheme will yet be successful in Pennsylvania is the hope of every citizen who has taken notice of this move in the interest of humanity. The old age pension bill has been bitterly fought by certain corporations in Pennsylvania, but just why there should be determined opposition to this measure, which was so earnestly espoused by Senator Albert Davis, of Lackawanna county and others, it is impossible to understand. Investigators who have been going about the state and making a study of the system can prove beyond a doubt that an old age pension law, which would be a boon to the unfortunate, would be a saving of expense to the commonwealth. It has long been well known that the cost of administering charity in Pennsylvania has been great. Salaried officials who dole out aid to the poor are **in most instances** paid sums far beyond what should be expended for this work. For instance, to care for a subject who could get along by himself if granted a pension of $10 a month requires at least four times that sum to keep him in any charitable institution in the state of Pennsylvania. If the salaried charity officials about the country were fighting the old age pension scheme it would not be so surprising, but to have the objection come from big corporations that would without doubt receive benefit in the reduction of poor taxes, is astounding indeed. An old age pension would reduce the poor taxes and it would give the unfortunate old people a feeling of independence that the frugal and thrifty should be allowed to enjoy in their declining years...

"One of the objections raised to the expediency, if not to the constitutionality of the bill, by the lawyers who were hired without the prospect of a pension themselves to question the constitutionality of the old age pension act, was that the act, if it were in force, would be paternalism, a vicious usurpation by the government of a "quasipaternal" relation to the citizen and his family. It seems to us that we have heard this verbage before. It is false, illogical and socially vicious. The relations of any government to the citizen and his family are of little or no consequence or value if they are not paternal. If they are nothing more than mechanical they are as inhuman and as soulless as a retaining wall over a dangerous railway embankment. It is the inhumanity, the undeviating mechanism of government, its soulless automatonism, which has given to socialism the moral and political ascendancy which it has already achieved and is potentially capable of achieving.... The man who said that the old age pensions 'are a vicious usurpation by the government of paternal relations to the citizen and his family' is a dangerous fool. He is intellectually atrophied" . . .

"The accumulation of wealth and the general welfare of society are not inconsistent, if wealth, whether in the form of corporate or individual interests, does not ignore its duties and is insistent merely upon what it calls its rights, those rights which are sanctified by legislation, not by morality. The danger to American capitalism does not arise from the disquietude of the proletariat, with the unequal and very often the iniquitous distribution of wealth, but through the insistence of capital to justify itself through archaic legislation—legislative enactments which dam up social progress. This is like choking up the outlets of the reservoir in rainy weather, it invites and encourages a dangerous inundation."

The Mirror—Altoona

"The fact that the Dauphin county court has declared Pennsylvania's old age pension act unconstitutional does not mean that the proposition is either dead or unconstitutional." . . .

"There is a general belief that the old age pension idea, is such an one as should be received with approval in every civilized and humanely disposed community. Thrift is a fine virtue, one which should be widely inculcated and universally adopted. But this life is full of unexpected vicissitudes. And the needy we have with us always and will have."

The Tribune— Reading

"James H. Maurer, the president of the State
Federation of Labor and the chairman of the State
Old Age Assistance Commission was justified in de-
nouncing the 'selfish minority which is attempting to
block' the execution of the old age assistance law
passed by the last legislature.' His stand will be
helpful if the people will get behind the movement
and demonstrate beyond question his claim that the
'public is for it.' . . .

"In the face of the figures, presented by Mr.
Maurer, the public cannot help but agree that 'it is
indeed ludicrous to accuse these people of 'improvidence' and 'gross negligence' to provide for their old
age.' They did not have even the conveniences and
comforts of life when they were working, as the
paucity of their wages evidence, and they could not
be expected to deprive themselves still further to pre-
pare for old age....How much better it would be to
keep the aged indigent at home where they feel that
they are still a part of society, any man who has ever
been fearful of the poorhouse can answer.

"The Old Age Assistance law, idealists have hoped,
is only a start in the proper direction. Old Age insurance, which would be coupled with compensation insurance, should be compulsory, allowing every working man and woman, after he or she has reached the
age of sixty-five, to retire in comfort and decency
for the remaining days. But if a selfish minority is
permitted to block the principal step in that direction,
what hope can the idealists hold out to faithful aged
citizens?"

The Tribune—Johnstown

"A Dauphin County judge finds the State Old
Age Assistance law is unconstitutional. . . The principle of the law is sound. . . We are not criticizing the
finding of the learned judge. He was elected to decide
such matters. We do say that if the State Constitution stands in the way of a sound Old Age Assistance
law, then the Constitution should be amended.

"Practically every large corporation has its pension
system. These pensions are now an accepted policy
of the large corporations. The need of such a system
grows as industry and business grow. The gathering together of great numbers of men and women in
combined effort for greater production brings the necessity of providing for the retirement of those who
become superannuated. It does not pay the big corporations to keep these on the payroll. It pays better
to pension them, This is outside of the sentimental
side of the problem. It is cold, hard business.

"But, there are other thousands who are not in such employment. The smaller employer cannot afford a pension system. The superannuated employee is just as great a drawback to the small employer as he is to the big corporation. Also, there are the thousands who have not been employees. The individual worker "for himself," and many others, becomes unable to earn a living. After years of honest effort and production which has gone to benefit the State and society—are these to be cast out, penniless, and sent to the poorhouse?

"Now, what is good for what some of our neighbors call "Big Business" ought to be good for little business. The world has been moving since our fathers made the present State Constitution. We have a compensation law which takes money from the public funds and gives it to individuals. It is constitutional. There is some difference between a compensation law and an old age pension law, we will admit—but it is a difference so small, in principle, that the layman can scarcely comprehend the learned judge's fine line of cleavage.

"The work of procuring an amendment to the Constitution should be started. . . If the big corporations can take the shareholders' money and pay it out in pensions to deserving employees, why cannot the State take the people's money and pay it out to equally deserving persons, who by long lives of honest toil have well earned this "assistance?"

___

The Sun—Williamsport

"The decision of the Dauphin County court declaring unconstitutional the old age pension act passed by the last legislature, is a surprise and disappointment to the supporters of the pension proposal."

___

The Tribune—Greensburg

"At the very beginning of old age pension legislation in this state it has been made clear that the only way to put it into effect is through an amendment to the state constitution. That it would be adopted if put up to the people is confidently believed. The idea is growing in other countries as well as in the United States and is regarded as a humane, as well as a wise measure of government."

___

Labor News—Beaver

Law, and it is to be hoped that Governor Pinchot, who signed the act making it a law, is correct in his prognostication that every other State in the Union will soon follow the good example set by the Keystone State. When it is conclusively demonstrated by facts and figures, as was done at the conference on Old Age Assistance at Harrisburg recently, that it is less expensive and more humane for a State to provide pensions for the destitute aged instead of sending them 'over the hills to the poorhouse,' the foundation is knocked from under the opposition of those who are still in favor of the dismal, inhuman and antiquated poorhouse system.

"In eleven years, from 1911 to 1922, forty American States and two territories enacted Mothers' Pension laws, despite strong opposition from certain sources, to keep poor children at home rather than send them to uncharitable 'charitable' institutions. Old Age pensions are only an extension of the same beneficient principle to keep families together where there are aged dependants.

"The tragedy of institutional childhood is no greater than the tragedy of institutionalized old age. Than the callous neglect of the gloomy and dehumanized poor-houses in this country, there is no sadder chapter in the social history of America. Complex modern industrial conditions seem to thrust aside the aged and incapacitated worker as a useless economic factor. Relatives or friends may not be able to provide for such helpless persons, and to provide pensions for these is now postively known to be much cheaper and better in every way than sending them to pass away their last days in poor-houses."

The Citizen—Honesdale

"The Pennsylvania Old Age Pension law has been declared unconstitutional, not on its merits or demerits as a good or bad law, but because the Constitution of Pennsylvania will not permit legislation of this sort....

"Doubtless the decision will renew the debates over the benefits or evils of a public pension system which raged while the bill was before the Legislature. . . . .

"But that aside, there are those who richly deserve something better than the poorhouse. Take, for example, the man of small ability who has worked as hard as he knows how to bring up a family or to care for helpless loved ones, and who, unable to save when he should have, comes down to the sunset of life with nothing put by for a rainy day. Or the woman who, as wife or widow, has slaved away the best years of her life and never has been so situated that she could save. For such as these the State can afford to be more than generous. These men and women have earned the right to a place in the sun in their old age; to ease and contentment and plenty in their declining years.

"Somewhere between the pension for everybody and careless disregard for really worthy folks, it would seem, lies the middle ground of common sense that everybody ought to map out for the rest of us to follow."

Gifford Pinchot—Governor of Pennsylvania

"I considered it a pleasure and privilege as Governor of this Commonwealth, to sign the Old Age Assistance Act, not only because our present system of poor-relief is antiquated and inadequate; not merely because an old age pension system is a much more economical method than the present inefficient and costly poorhouse system, but also, because I am convinced that the men and women who have helped, by their brain and brawn, to give to this Commonwealth the prosperity we are all enjoying, and who have reared families who continue their honest and productive labor have contributed sufficiently to our Commonwealth as to be entitled to a somewhat more serene and happier life in their declining days than the heart-rending wretchedness we are according them today in our almshouses. It has given me profound pleasure to sign this bill. Today we are righting the neglects of yesterday. As Governor of this Commonwealth, I am proud that ours is the first industrial state to adopt the law. Other states will soon see the wisdom of our procedure and enact similar legislation to make happier the lot of the aged within their borders. The highest duty of humanity is to care for those who have served the glory of the State and the nation as well, and as loyally as they knew how."

William C. Sproul—Former Governor of Pennsylvania

"I am glad to hear that you are getting on well with your work and I trust that something may be evolved which will be practical and attainable."

Martin G. Brumbaugh—Former Governor of Pennsylvania

"You know my interest and deep concern in the Old Age Assistance Commission. The members are all admirably equipped for a great service and the purpose of the Commission I heartily approve. May you have great success."

W. Freeland Kendrick—Mayor of Philadelphia

"I am deeply interested in any worthy enterprise which has for its purpose the inherent duty to care for the poor, and I wish to extend to you and your associates who are working so zealously for the procuring of a greater measure of justice to our dependent aged, a word of encouragement."

Hugh Gilmore—Mayor of Williamsport

"My sympathies are with you in this grand work. I know of many aged poor who are struggling for an existence and are in pitiful circumstances but too proud to beg and I surely voice not only my sentiments but the majority of our people, when I say, God speed the day when this proposed law is working satisfactorily and aiding these needy unfortunates."

Rt. Rev. James H. Darlington—Harrisburg

"I am heartily in favor of Old Age Assistance."

Rt. Rev. M. J. Hoban—Scranton

"I am heartily in favor of the principle of Old Age Assistance. The accepted principle of keeping the family together should hold even when the family has been reduced to poverty through no fault of theirs.

"Over the hills to the poor-house is a most pathetic journey for the man or woman, who may have served the community to the best of his or her ability, led upright lives and then were broken on the wheel of fortune.

"I sincerely hope that the Supreme Court may consider the spirit rather than the letter of the Constitution and declare the Old Age Act constitutional."

Rt. Rev. Francis J. McConnell—Pittsburgh

"The proper care of the old in ways that will discharge society's obligation to them without harming their self respect is a most urgent duty."

Rt. Rev. Ethelbert Talbot—Bethlehem

"It is a disgrace to our Christian civilization that a more considerate and humane provision has not been made hitherto for the comfort of those who are overtaken with misfortune and dependent in their old age."

Mrs. Ella George, President, Woman's Christian Temperance Union of Pennsylvania

"I am in hearty sympathy with your object. It saddens the heart of one who has a sympathetic human touch to learn of old people, who perhaps through no fault of their own, had been reduced to poverty. I do hope that the Bill may not be declared unconstitutional by the Supreme Court."

William Draper Lewis, Formerly Dean of University of Pennsylvania Law School

"There is no more important thing in this State at the present time than the work on which you are engaged. For much more than one hundred years the State has recognized some obligation to those who, having worked hard during their active lives, find themselves destitute in old age. That there are many such is a reflection on our economic and business organization, but the fact exists and imposes on the people of Pennsylvania as represented in their State government a positive duty. How much better is it to fulfill this duty by a system of pensions such as your Commission has recommended than by contributions to almshouses and similar institutions which not only unjustly put the stigma of receiving charity on many deserving old persons, but often care for those who, if they were in receipt of a small monthly stipend, would remain in their homes without being an undue burden on relatives, friends and neighbors."

Dr. Francis D. Tyson, Professor of Economics—University of Pittsburgh

"It is incredible that our Commonwealth should longer delay the granting of assistance to the dependent aged, —a belated measure of public justice undertaken by our sister nation, Great Britain, more than fifteen years ago. The significant Old Age Assistance Act of Pennsylvania constitutes us a leader among the states in such legislation."

The Late William Flinn—Former State Senator—Pittsburgh

"The Old Age Penison proposition is full of merit and justice."

Judge Harry H. Rowand, Court of Common Pleas—Pittsburgh

"I have read this bill carefully, and to my mind it is a model piece of proposed legislation."

Guy E. Campbell, Member of the National Congress, 32nd District, Pa.

"I am in hearty accord with the good work of the Old Age Pension Commission."

Steven G. Porter, Congressman at Large, Pennsylvania

"I believe that modern industrial and social conditions demand the passage of an Old Age Pension Law,

John M. Morin, Congressman at Large, Pennsylvania

"I wish to say that Pennsylvania, in passing the Old Age Pension Bill, is answering the query 'Am I my brother's keeper?' by action rather than words. The friends of humanitarian legislation everywhere will take courage in advocating the consideration of human rights as the most important of governmental functions."

During the discussions of The Old Age Assistance Bill, a number of Senators and representatives also stated their attitude towards this Act as follows:

Wm. S. Vare, Former State Senator, Philadelphia

"I deem it an honor to sponsor this bill. A pension for the aged is not an Utopian theory—it is a practical necessity."

Albert Davis—State Senator, Scranton

"I am in favor of an old age pension. We have statistics to prove, beyond a doubt, that the saving will pay more than the extra money it takes to provide for these people. It costs as much money to keep those paupers in the poor houses as it will under their own roofs, and I am sure that the State of Pennsylvania has always responded to humanitarian legislation. This, to my mind, is the greatest piece of legislation ever presented to this body and I am sure today that a majority of the Senate will vote for this bill. I used this argument in my campaign and I owe it to my people...

"I recall an incident which occurred in Berks County. The Chairman of the Commission investigating the Old Age Pension made a visit to the Berks County Almshouse and walking up the lane he met two old people, husband and wife. They approached the gate of the poorhouse at the same time. The superintendent asked 'what do you desire?' They answered: 'We have a permit to enter the poor farm.' That is very consoling to every man in the Senate. The superintendent asked 'What is your name?' 'My name is John.' 'And your name?' 'My name is Mary.' The superintendent said 'John, you go to the building over there, and Mary you go to that building over there.' John said 'What After living under the same roof for fifty years are we now going to be separated?' 'Yes, those are the rules, males on the one side, and the females on the other.' And—what happened? A tragedy. Three days after John entered that door he passed away with a broken heart and only a few days later his wife passed away with a broken heart." . . .

T. Larry Eyre, State Senator, Chester

"We must do everything possible to remove the stigma of pauperism from our worthy aged men and women."

Henry E. Lanius, State Senator, York

"This Pension Fund is not a proposition of dollars and cents. . . Where do we get the idea of the almshouse? We get it from the Elizabethan age. It showed us the policy of taking care of the poor. There we followed England. We followed Europe in its compensation act. We followed them in the child labor laws. Europe tried this old age pension and I am not prepared to believe that they think it is a failure,; I am not prepared to believe that the German people believe it is a failure. As a matter of fact, I get reports from Germany and England, that as a matter of economy, this is a good system; and so far as saying it will take away the incentive for men to do something, that they will say some may look forward and say 'Oh well, it doesn't matter what I do, sixty or seventy-five years from now I will be eligible for a pension,' I do not believe that will be the case. Mr. President, that is foolish, I say to you there is enough of Americanism which will make him refuse a pension. We can well afford as Pennsylvanians to put into practice some of that wonderful service we are always talking about. The History of this nation, the history of this world, is written in service and humanity and kindness, it is not written in oppression, or dollars and cents."

Horace W. Schanz, State Senator, Lehigh

"I consider this a meritorious measure, right in principle, economically sound and an act of simple justice. The Senate Appropriations Committee is certain that the Vare bill will greatly reduce the number of poorhouses, that the savings will far outweigh the expense to the state."

Herman Dilsheimer, State Representative, Philadelphia

"To my estimation, I don't believe there has been a bill presented to us of more importance and more human purpose than this bill."....

Miss Helen Grimes, State Representative, Pittsburgh

"On general principles I am opposed to the pension scheme, but there are three kinds of pensions which I believe in. One of those is a pension for soldiers, men who have been drafted into service of this country and have fought for it. The other one is for widows whose comfort."......

rren C. Harer, State Representative, Williamsport
"This Old Age Pension legislation affects the very foundation of the progress of our Commonwealth."

eph C. Marcus, State Representative, Pittsburgh
"I have listened with considerable interest to the remarks wherein the question of human lives and the Almighty Dollar has been compared.....I would ask any member of this House to name me one particular measure that has meant much to the State that has not required many years of study and investigation and expenditure of money.....

"I hope that every man and woman in this House will vote for this bill, from a standpoint that those that we love and those that we hold dearest to our hearts may become beneficiaries of this bill and let us look forward to the time when Pennsylvania will play its part in protecting those who have become unfortunate."......

seph G. Steedle, State Representative, McKees Rocks
"I hope the members of this House will not delay a so-important, a so-humanitarian piece of legislation. To my mind it is one of the best things that has come before this House from the standpoint of humanity."..

CHAPTER IX.

HE PENNSYLVANIA CONFERENCE ON OI AGE ASSISTANCE

e Pennsylvania Conference on Old Age Assistance, the fi ind in the United States, called by the State Old Age Assis mission was held on November 13th, 1924, at the Capitol tion to delegates from local old age assistance boards from hundred people in attendance, representing about thirty different organizations in the State. Says the American Labor Legislation Review:—"Never were the economies of statewide old age pensions contrasted more effectively with the wastefulness of the antiquated poorhouse system than at the Pennsylvania Conference on Old Age Assistance."

On account of the limited space, we are unfortunately unable to print in full the important addresses delivered before this Conference. However, the speeches made by Governor Pinchot and Chairman Maurer have been embodied in the main report. In view of the significant material presented by the other speakers, we must at least present summaries of these.

WHAT OUR BOARD HAS LEARNED FROM 100 APPLICATIONS

JAMES F. COLLIER.

Chairman Lycoming County Old Age Assistance Board

Some years ago I was asked by a friend to assist him with my car in taking an aged couple to the almshouse, and on the way there 1 heard the old couple speak to one another and say that at last they would not have to worry any more about where their meals came from, and seemed to be quite satisfied with their lot. When we arrived at the institution, the wife and husband, after going through some little formal routine, were taken to different parts of the building and in calling back to see the old lady I was simply astonished to find her in tears, and wondered why it was that she and her aged husband who had lived together for almost fifty years should at this time be separated when the grave was about to receive them both. I, of course, was helpless to assist these people, but I learned afterwards that through the kindness of some friends in their locality they were brought back home and placed both under the same roof and taken care of until their death. It occurred to me at that time that if ever there was a law passed which would keep two old souls of this kind together and permit them to die in peace in one another's arms, if possible, I would be highly in favor of it, and when the Old Age Assistance Act was brought up, it occurred to me that this was the very thing that would fill this bill.

It is said by a Life Insurance Company that the laws of averages work out very nicely in 100 lives, and as your Board from my County have acted in 99 lives, we feel rather certain that it will give a pretty fair idea of conditions. We find that of these 99, 87 were approved, 11 were rejected and one was withdrawn. We also find that three have answered that last summons since making application, and we sincerely trust that they have found a home better than the one they had on this earth. The average amount of assistance granted each applicant per month is $24.36. We find that there were 97 white people and there was one negro; 71 of these were men and 27 were women.

The argument that this Act would reward the shiftless and unworthy is absolutely without foundation and contrary to the facts. First, no shiftless and unworthy have applied in Lycoming County. Were any such to apply, their claims would be investigated and if found to have no means of support and no children able to care for them no doubt they would be afforded assistance, as they would become public charges if denied such assistance under the Act and sent to the almshouse to be supported out of the public moneys at a possibly greater cost than that offered by the Old Age Assistance Law. Furthermore, it is the case in Lycoming County as, no doubt, it is the case in other counties that the Assistance Board has been organized by placing a man in the western end of the County, one in the Central part of the County, and another in the eastern end. These men from their very long residence in their locality are acquainted with practically all of the applicants, and those whom they did not know a great deal about, they made inquiries concerning, thereby removing the possibility of caring for shiftless persons.

Right here, let me ask if we must neglect people in their old age because they happen to be shiftless in early life? Is it charitable to permit a man or woman to die of want because they happen to make some mistakes in their earlier lives?

Speaking of charity, I feel that if a man or woman were totally devoid of such a quality, and he made a trip of investigation with the members of the Lycoming County Board, he or she would have generated in them some of this virtue of charity before they had finished. . . .Very often a great many of us use the word "shiftless" when the word "unfortunate" would be more to the point; and right here I wish to make a statement concerning an ex-member of our own legislature who served a term here in Harrisburg as a member of the House and who is now applying for Old Age Assistance. The man is eighty years old. I have personally known him for a quarter of a century and I know that he endeavored to do what he could during his life in order that he might have some accumulation for old age, but 80 years is quite a good while to round out, and now he finds himself and his wife in destitute circumstances, he being too old to work although he has tried to work within the last year, and who will dare say that this man was shiftless?

In order not to be too harsh on people who are poor in their old age, let me say to you that, according to statistics gotten up by a very prominent Life Insurance Company on 100 healthy lives at age 25, the following has happened to them when they reached 65:—

One was rich;
Four were wealthy;
Five were still in the harness working for their daily bread;
Thirty-six were gone to their final account;
And 54 were dependent upon others for a livelihood.

How then, are we going to blame the aged poor or avoid caring for them?

Now, with respect to reckless spending of the grant by the beneficiaries, I ask anyone here if there could be any reckless spending from $1.00 per day. I am informed by the Deputy Sheriff of Lycoming County that it costs 50 cents per day to keep the prisoners, people who have committed sins against society. Yet this Act only allows a maximum of $1.00 a day from which the recipient must pay rent, heat, light, medicine and live. To my mind this argument of reckless spending is simply absurd. The grant is not of sufficient largeness to admit of reckless spending.

Judging from the character of applicants received by the Lycoming County Board, they have, without exception, been persons who never were addicted to reckless spending. The contention is further made by the opponents of this Act that it would remove the burden of support from children who are able but unwilling to support their parents. You will note that we handled cases of this kind in Williamsport and rejected a man because his children were able to support him, and we also notified the children of our action. Another case which we held up on account of feeling that the son of the applicant was able to support his parent was taken up with the son. He wrote us to remove the application, feeling no doubt that he intended to try to take care of his old parent, but by a personal investigation made by the Lycoming County Board and verified through a visit by Mr. Epstein proved that this man was unable to take care of his father.

You will therefore see, ladies and gentlemen, that at least one County in this Commonwealth has proved by earnest, insistent, conscientious, careful and painstaking investigation that this Old Age Assistance Law would not reward the shiftless and unworthy; it would not remove the burden of support from children who are able but unwilling to support their parents and above all, it would not cause reckless spending of the grant by the beneficiaries. We are positive that when the balance of the aged poor in Lycoming County have been located, the same conditions will prevail amongst them as has prevailed amongst the first hundred.

WHY PUBLIC SENTIMENT IN OUR COUNTY IS SOLIDLY BEHIND OLD AGE ASSISTANCE.

MRS. W. B. GRAY

Secretary, Beaver County Old Age Assistance Board.

Beaver County is solidly behind the Old Age Assistance Act. Men and women representatives of all classes and social strata in our county with whom I had an opportunity to talk about the subject are all agreed upon the superiority of this humane method of care of the dependent aged over that of the disgraceful county home. Public sentiment in our county is behind this law for the following reasons:

1. Because we think old age assistance represents economy in government.

2. Because it allows the old people to live at home and take care of themselves when they can, rather than the inhuman plan of separating an aged couple after spending a life-time together.

3. The fact that judges, teachers and state employees have pension systems in operation under State laws, we cannot understand why people who had rendered just as vital services, should not also be provided with some comforts in old age.

4. Because it is a true American principle and desire to maintain one's independence to the end of his days. And many old people without any blame to them are poor and unable to maintain their homes, but, who, with a little help, could live independent lives,

5. Because no institution or county home can take the place of our own home. I know, from personal observation of both public and church institutions, that even if they furnish everything necessary for the comfort of the body, yet the spirit of home is lacking. We believe that the state is entirely justified in assisting the aged citizens to maintain their own home where-ever possible, and that it would be but paying back a little to those who helped to make the state possible.

From my experience with over 100 applicants, most of whom I have investigated personally, I find that a great many of these had no education and never learned a trade and when they became old, the manufacturers found no place for them. Their children are married and scattered, each struggling to maintain their own existence and unable to assist their aged parents.

I have had an application of a man who worked twenty-eight years in one steel plant. Without any notice whatsoever he was told one pay day that his services were no longer needed. He expected to be pensioned in two years. Imagine the disappointment of that man! He had worked for small wages, had a large family, his sons and daughters were married and have all they can do to maintain their own homes. He is failing in health and too old to get work. It is for people of this kind that Beaver County is willing to work and fight for an adequate old age assistance plan.

Another old lady who was left a widow with a large family to take care of, has four daughters, who are all widows with large families of their own; one son a cripple, one an invalid and not one able to contribute a dollar toward her support. She is past seventy and is not able to do any work. We say the county home is no place for this woman. A little old age assistance would help to provide her with, at least, one room which would be a real "home."

For these and numerous other reasons, which, if time permitted, I could cite, we are heartily in favor of this great measure undertaken by the State. We have fifty-three approved applications, all of which have been carefully investigated. To stop our work at this time would not only be unfortunate, but would also mean a waste of the State's money which has already been spent in the gathering of the data which has been carried on vigorously. Let us, therefore, all work with more zeal for a new and more adequate law for old age assistance.

OLD AGE ASSISTANCE AN IMPROVEMENT OVER THE POOR HOUSE.

MRS. JANET WORKMAN

Secretary, Washington County Old Age Assistance Board

It is not necessary for any one to be a member of a County Old Age Assistance Board in order to become aware of the superiority of a system of old age assistance to aged folks as against sending these unfortunate aged "over the hill to the poor house." Anyone who has known an aged person, faced with this prospect, after a lifetime of toil and struggle, is fully conscious of the dread and bitterness with which his life is filled. No one, who has ever been inside of a county home, can fail to realize the advantages, from every point of view, of a system of aid in their own homes over even the best managed almshouses.

All through my work, as secretary of the Washington County Old Age Assistance Board, it has been borne upon me that the prospects of the poorhouse with its stigma of pauperism is so detestable to the honest, though poor man and woman, that they would rather go through the greatest sufferings and anguishes of heart, than accept this charity. The aged man and woman does not wish to give up the long-established home ties, life associations, nor to loose sight of the old home and to hear no longer the sound of their loved ones' voices. They do not want to be set apart and compelled to live the depressing and uneventful life, generally prevailing even in the best managed almshouse. It is but natural that after many years of activity and independence when they have been "lords of their own castles" that the aged man or woman should desire to be let alone and permitted to continue to manage his or her own affairs, and to live within the home circle, amidst which he spent the greater part of his life. It is hardly fair to expect of the aged man and woman to break the habits of a lifetime and accept cheerfully the serenity of an institution. That the institution is not the best place, even for children, we have recognized long ago by our adoption of a Mothers' Assistance Fund, and in the present aim everywhere to place children in private homes rather than in institutions. Why should it be expected, then, that the aged man or woman should find the institution a fitter place to live in?

That the almshouse does not provide that serenity of life which it was originally intended to give has been made clear by the Old Age Pension Commission after its studies of conditions in our county institutions throughout the State. I wonder if there is anyone with red blood flowing in his or her veins who has loved his or her father or mother that can contemplate, without outrageous indignation, the separation of someone else's loving father or mother in different parts of the poorhouse after a life of fifty or sixty years together and at a period when they need each other's care most?

It is a well known fact that our entire system of poor relief and almshouse care are antiquated institutions, relics of a civilization long past, totally unsuited to modern conditions and which should have been overhauled many years ago. Our poor laws dating back over three hundred years, and the needs long having outgrown the almshouse as an effective institution, it is almost difficult to conceive that we could have gone on until this day with the instruments provided three hundred years ago, practically unchanged. This is even more puzzling when is is remembered that our very poor laws, which have originated in England, have long ago been overhauled in the mother country and new methods instituted. Originally intended as a place where the decrepit aged may find comfort in their declining days and some employment when able to do so, the almshouse to day has become instead a place of refuge for all unfortunates, and the dreaded spectre of all.

The general impression that our poor houses represent the cheapest and most economical method of care of the dependent aged is certainly without foundation. The only explanation of this belief is the fact that, until very recently there was no adequate system of accounting provided in calculating the cost of maintaining the poor, to the county or township. As the Old Age Pension Commission stated in the already referred to Report,:— "The State supervision of these aged homes is insufficient, loose and hardly competent. Careful records are kept in only few institutions. There is no uniform method of accounting. Computations of costs are made in almost as many forms and methods as the men making them. Many of the per capita costs of almshouses given in the reports of the Board of Public Charities do not represent the actual cost. The latter do not include the interest upon the permanent investment and, in many cases, do not include the value of farm products."

Thus, for instance, in the case of my own county, the Commission found that while the average per capita per week in 1917, as given by the poor directors to the Board of Public Charities, was $2.03, the Commission's figures based on the total expenditures made that year and divided by the number of days support in the institution showed a weekly expenditure of $8.76 per capita, or approximately $35.00 per month.

In 1923, the average daily per capita cost in Washington County is reported to the Department of Public Welfare as amounting to 76 cents, or $5.32 per week. That this figure, however, does not represent the real cost to the county of supporting an inmate in our county home is clearly apparent when it is noted that in the total almshouse expense of $67,934.30, as given by the Directors of the Poor for that year, no item of the produce raised on the county farm and consumed in the home, is included. Obviously, the fact that 150 acres of farm land are under cultivation and that but little of the products raised are sold outside, would if properly accounted, add considerably to the total expenditures.

Furthermore, no mention is made in this total in regard to the interest upon the permanent investment involved, which although from the view point of any sound business man, must always be reckoned as part of the expenditures, seem at no time to be considered in the case of our county institutions. The investments embodied in the land and buildings of our country farm are estimated at least, at $350,000. Even five per cent interest on this investment gives a total of $17,500 per year, which must be added to the expenditures of the county home. When this is divided by the 211 inmates in the home, $83.00 per year, or $1.59 per week, must be added to the per capita cost of every inmate. Thus, the total weekly per capita cost of supporting an inmate in the Washington County Home, with only five per cent interest on the permanent investment added, but no account still being taken of the food consumed from the County Farm, amounts really to $6.91, or in round figures, $7.00 per week, rather than the $5.32 given by the County Controller. It is this price, at least, that we pay for separating an aged man from his beloved wife and for imposing the odious stigma of pauperism upon him. And it is this $7.00 weekly per capita cost in our almshouse that we must contrast with the average allowance of $21.43 per month, per applicant, made so far by our County Old Age Assistance Board.

Again, in 1923, according to the report submitted by the Directors of the Poor to the Department of Public Welfare, $14,538.00 of a total almshouse expense of $67,934.30, or practically 21.5 per cent

7g

was spent on "Salaries and Expenses" alone, exclusive of all other overhead charges; in other words, $21.50 of every $100.00 appropriated for the poor in the almshouse was spent in paying the men for delivering this money. In the five months our Board has been in existence, we spent, up to Oct. 10th, a total overhead expense of $12.70. For this munificient sum, we have been able to check up and to act upon 70 applications, most of which need not be re-investigated when money becomes available, granting allowances to 61 persons, up to a total of $15,684.00 per year. THUS, UNDER THE OLD AGE ASSISTANCE ACT, WE HAVE BEEN ABLE TO CARRY ON OUR BUSINESS AT AN OVERHEAD EXPENSE TO THE COUNTY OF LESS THAN EIGHT CENTS PER HUNDRED DOLLARS DISTRIBUTED, WHILE, IN THE CASE OF THE ALMSHOUSE, THIS SAME OVERHEAD IS $21.48 PER HUNDRED DOLLARS; OR 268 TIMES AS MUCH. The State's expense in administering this money from that end, judging from the budget asked by the Commission for the next biennium, is actually below what it cost the State today in supervising the County Homes through the Bureau of Maintenance in the Department of Public Welfare.

I am not citing the above figures as of peculiar credit to our County Board. I have no doubt, and the Secretary of the State Commission assures me that it is so, that approximately the same small overhead percentages exist in a number of other counties. I am referring to these only to show that they are inherent in the Old Age Assistance Act. Once the State adopts a more just method of treatment for the less fortunate members of society, there will always be plenty of persons who will gladly and cheerfully assume duties and burdens and give as much of their time and energies as possible, regardless of financial considerations. It is one thing to be a Director of the Poor and be compelled to shatter the lives of aged persons by sending them to almshouses, but one is honored as a member of a County Old Age Assistance Board, through which he or she can help to make the declining days of an aged person somewhat happier. Thus, the Old Age Assistance Act is not only a superior and more humanely just instrument of meeting the needs of the dependent aged than the antiquated poor house, but it is even economically a far less expensive method. For these reasons, I trust, the Supreme Court will see its justice and sustain the Act.

THE SIGNIFICANCE OF THE PENNSYLVANIA OLD AGE ASSISTANCE ACT IN THE UNITED STATES.

· DR. JOHN B. ANDREWS
Secretary, American Association for Labor Legislation.

A great impetus was given to the movement for statewide old age pensions in America when, a year ago, an industrial state of the first magnitude—Pennsylvania—enacted an enlightened law for old age assistance. The Pennsylvania act, together with the old age pension laws of Montana and Nevada enacted in the same year, mark a significant forward step in American social legislation. It may be said with assurance that old age pensions have now reached the pioneering stage with respect to legislative adoption that mothers' pensions had reached a dozen years ago. Now that a beginning has been made we may look for state after state to fall.in line.

In the eleven years—1911 to 1921—forty American states and two territories enacted mothers' pension laws to keep children in the home rather than in institutions. Old age pension laws are an extension of the same principle to keep families together where theré are aged dependents. The tragedy of institutionalized childhood is no greater than the tragedy of institutionalized old age. To tear an old veteran of industry away from wife or children or chronies after a life time of honest toil and commit him to the uncertain care of strangers in a strange place is so inhuman an aspect of our industrial civilization that it is certain to be everywhere remedied.

A determining argument in behalf of mothers' pension legislation was the practical experience which shows it is better to pay the mother for taking care of her children in her home than to spend the same amount in financing institutions, in even the best of which care is unsatisfactory and the death rate is abnormally high. So with old age pensions—the straight old age pension, as embodied in the three pioneer state laws, in the recently extended law of Alaska, and in a standard bill to aid further state legislation, is, because of its simplicity of administration, more economical than any other plan. There is perhaps no sadder chapter in American social history than the callous neglect in dehumanized poorhouses for the care of aged dependents.

Complex modern industry thrusts aside the aged or incapacitated worker as a useless economic factor. Relatives or friends may not be able or willing to carry the burden. A dark prospect confronts an increasing number of faithful workers. Existing private pension systems are an insignificant factor in meeting the need.

Charity care is inefficient and bad, although large sums are expended. The issue is home instead of institutional care. The purpose is to ease off the last days of our old men and women, who have contributed all their productive lives to industry and national well-being, in the same spirit with which we now pension off the aged judges, generals and other public servants in city, state and nation. The economical and humane method is by means of a well organized statewide system of old age pensions. As a practical solution this will be most satisfactory to the aged dependents, more economical for our industries, and best for the community.

SOCIAL RESPONSIBILITY FOR OLD AGE DEPENDENCY.
DR. I. M. RUBINOW

Director, Jewish Welfare Society of Philadelphia.

To a student of social conditions a very interesting problem presents itself—why this antagonism to Old Age Assistance legislation—why these stubborn efforts to negate the will of the people as expressed in the legislative enactment—why this appeal to a sentence in the constitution whose meaning is uncertain? Surely, the American people at large and particularly the more prosperous strata are not at all neglectful of the needs of the aged. Hundreds of thousands of old men and women are supported in private or

public institutions, other hundreds of thousands, receive
less generous public or private outdoor relief.

The War Pension System which before the World War w
ing more than a selective old age pension system has al
ceived generous support from Congress. In appeals for pr
nevolence for various Federation drives the needs of the
and women are always emphasized together with the needs
dren. The necessary emotional reaction is therefore availal
very individuals who are fighting the Pennsylvania Old Ag
ance Act may contribute generously to the Federation dr
I may indulge in a bit of psychology I believe I can offer the
ation. The need is fully realized and acknowledged.
resented is the principle underlying Old Age Assistance,
social responsibility for the needs of old age in present societ

Society, or at least that part of it which for some reason
has the largest share in the advantages of the modern s
production, is not heartless; it readily admits the existen
pendency, it readily admits the necessity of coming to assis
does. What it resents is the admission that society, meani
selves, is responsible for the situation. It is natural for
vidual who is inadequate, who is a failure, to blame societ
failure. He transfers the responsibility from himself to tl
around him, because that is the only consolation left as he
know how to meet his own problems. It is equally nat
society at large to blame the individual for a transgressior
ure, so as to relieve its own sense or responsibility. One n
it is the natural pastime of "passing the buck".

The important question is—who can meet the situation
dividual or the whole social organism, and whoever that
is socially responsible.

The problem of Old Age Dependency is a problem of the
industrial area, is a problem of large cities, it is a problem
from destruction of the patriarchal family. It is a proble
chine production, industrial efficiency—The Taylor System.
result of the Wage System, industrial competition, and etc.

Surely, all of these are social conditions that can be mo
corrected only through social action, and that after all is
important meaning of "Social Responsibility".

How can the individual meet the problem of Old Age?
modern industrial system presupposes magnates of indus
presupposes incomes running into millions, it is only beca
predicated upon millions of wage earners. Manufacturing
alone employs nearly fifteen million people, but the total n
manufacturers and officials, and managers, and even superi
does not exceed one-half million. There are over three
people in transportation, but less than twenty thousand
Trade and commerce remains the most individual of occ
but even there, out of nearly five million people, less than
lion at most are either in the employing or in the independ
e. Add to it millions of clerical employees, mining, and far
the number of wage workers surely exceeds twenty-five
people. It is their problem that old age assistance plans
cerned with. Who is responsible for their becoming a prol
time when they are beyond their working capacity?. Sure
not seriously claim that men and women over 70 years o

to compete successfully in modern industry, transpor-
merce; and so long as our life preservation movement
e successful as it has been, so long will this problem
:rease. To deny social responsibility for the situation,
ividual responsibility as an explanation also means to
idual action as a remedy. What form can such in-
n take?
·aving is a remedy proposed. Is this remedy adequate?
·ages even in New York in manufacturing industries
t $27 a week. What particular study of cost of living
ted that this average income out of which a family
, provides for a surplus out of which old age provision
? A method to make such savings would be an effort
tion of the standards of living of twenty-five millions.
assume for a moment that notwithstanding the rise
living, such economies and such reduction of standard
ible. I wonder what the result would be upon a whole
tem of such wholesale reduction in consumption.
y, not even to raise the question, what would become of
onditions of life if everything but bare necessity is

problem of Old Age has been obviously discussed in
he last twenty-years. Mr. Epstein's very effective study
)ld Age" is one of the latest contributions. Books,
.d reports on the subject in my library date back to
In the bulky study made by the state of Massachu-
or 1908, the theory was advanced that old age depend-
a social but a family responsibility, that old age pen-
ving the family of this responsibility, would break up
: family solidarity, but every experienced family case
s there is nothing that contributes so much to the
odern family as the additional responsibility and weight
ie older generation, in addition to the rearing of chil-
seless to apply ideals which have grown in a large New
ι house to conditions of a modern working man's home
y. Life insurance has reached a stupendous dimension
ecause with the break-up of the patriarcal family, the
s and orphans became a social responsibility. Mothers'
veloped out of the condition as even life insurance was
et the problem of widowhood and orphanage for mil-
workers. Real Estate and Bond Investments are the
.l effective way of meeting the problem of superannua-
ié well-to-do. It is puerile to offer the same recommen-
millions of wage workers. BY THE PROCESS OF
, OLD AGE ASSISTANCE REMAINS THE ONLY
METHOD
ι time when excessive cost was raised as a serious ob-
·as seriously argued in England that the cost of Old
would ruin the British exchequer. Three years later
ι was spending every day for purposes of destruction
e annual cost of the Old Age Pension System. One

WHAT WILL BECOME OF THE ALMSHOUSES?

DR. ELLEN C. POTTER

Secretary, Pennsylvania Department of Welfare

In a letter addressed to the Conference, Dr. Potter declared:

"The question has been presented to us as to what would become of the almshouses and County Homes in Pennsylvania if the aged were to be provided for through pension grants in their own homes.

"To a person who has been watching the trend in the field of poor law administration the answer seems obvious, based upon the change in the character of the almshouse population during the last ten years.

"The well constructed county home will continue but it will function more as a county hospital for the care of the chronically ill and infirm who cannot be taken care of even on a pension in their own homes or in boarding homes.

"We receive requests for information frequently as to what can be done by the Directors on behalf of certain of their charges who cannot be taken care of properly in the county homes as they are now equipped. On the other hand many of our hospitals for the care of the acutely ill find their wards clogged with chronic cases who can no longer be benefitted by treatment and, who, nevertheless, need care in an institution for incurables.

"It is, therefore, obvious that if our county homes were so equipped and officered as to provide care for the chronically sick and the infirm they would meet a very great need in the community, while at the same time the aged who are physically able to live outside in their own or boarding homes could be provided for by pensions."

The Eagles' Campaign

John F. O'Toole, Chairman of the Pennsylvania Old Age Pension Commission of the Fraternal Order of Eagles reveiwed the activities of the Eagles in this legislation throughout the country and the State, declared the fight for Old Age Pensions which is now part of the organic law of the Order will not be relinquished and there will be no turning back until old age assistance laws are established throughout the country.

Labor Will Fight On

Thomas Kennedy, President, District No. 7, and recently elected Secretary-Treasurer of the United Mine Workers of America, speaking for organized labor, declared that the labor movement in the State is determined to fight for an adequate old age assistance act to the utmost of its energies: He declared that the working man and woman who have helped in the building up of our industries, contributed to our own welfare and raised families who continue to do the hard work of society, are, even as judges and teachers, entitled to some better care in their old age than by casting them into the poorhouse with all societies' outcasts. "There will be no slackening in labor's fight for this law," declared Mr. Kennedy.

The Churches for Old Age Assistance

Rev. Wm. L. Mudge, Executive Secretary of the Pennsylvania Federation of Churches, representing more than a million Protestant church members in the State, declared that the churches are solidly behind the Old Age Assistance Law and will do their utmost in helping to promote the cause. "The home", he stated, "is the unit of civilization and all movements which tend to maintain the unity of the family, are invincible."

County Commissioners Endorse Old Age Assistance

Nathan F. Walker, Commissioner of Bradford County, and formerly President, State Association of County Commissioners, was unable to deliver his address in person but sent the following words:
"I am in favor of the Old Age Assistance, for when a man and wife have lived together for years and become needy, it is a shame to send them to the poor house. The poor house should be only for old people that are alone in this world and for others who are feeble minded and do not know how to care for themselves."
Previous to that, in October 1923, the Thirty-seventh Annual Convention of the Pennsylvania State Association of County Commissioners adopted the following resolution:

"Whereas, we were just accorded the opportunity of listening to a thorough discussion by Mr. A. Epstein, Executive Secretary of the Old Age Assistance Commission, in regard to the Old Age Assistance Act passed by the 1923 Legislature, and
"Whereas, we found the discussion valuable and enlightening, therefore

"Be it resolved, That the 37th Annual Convention of the State Association of County Commissioners of Pennsylvania hereby goes on record as endorsing the principle of Old Age Assistance to worthy and deserving aged persons in Pennsylvania, and expressing its desire to co-operate with the Old Age Assistance Commission in every manner possible."

Brief talks were also made by Bishop James H. Darlington, Harrisburg; Seibert Witman, member, Berks County Old Age Assistance Board and David S. Ludlum, Old Age Assistance Commissioner. The following accounts of their work were given by the guests from other states:

THE WORK OF THE MASSACHUSETTS COMMIS-SION ON PENSIONS.

EDMUND S. COGSWELL

Secretary, Massachusetts Commission on Pensions

The members of the Massachusetts' Commission appreciate the courtesy of the Pennsylvania Commission in extending an invitation to attend this helpful and very instructive conference, and Mr. C. J. Mahoney and myself, who represent the Commission, have derived much benefit from being in attendance.

As a result of old age pension bills before our Legislature of 1923, a commission was appointed consisting of five members to study the problem of old age pensions, ascertain the probable number who would be entitled to pensions under any system the commission may recommend and to estimate the cost.

The commission has held eight hearings on the subject of old age pensions in Massachusetts' cities and towns, and as a result of the publicity given to the hearings by newspapers, secretaries of chambers of commerce, labor unions, and others—the hearings have been well attended. Most of the speakers before the commission have favored old age pensions.

The commission has deemed it very essential to secure information about the condition of persons not now receiving public pensions or public or private organized charity. Nearly 20,000 persons, 65 years of age and over, have been interviewed in 34 cities and towns in Massachusetts and the statistics of the commission when tabulated will yield some very interesting information.

The Commissioner of Public Welfare of Massachusetts, has advised the Commission that in his opinion very few aged persons are sent to the almshouses for reasons of poverty alone, as practically all of those in the almshouse have physical or mental defects and need institutional care. The Commission's investigation has largely confirmed this statement. While no general rule has been adopted for the state as a whole, the practice in many cities and towns is to grant outdoor relief if the cost is not too high.

The usual per capita cost of maintaining an almshouse inmate is about $7 per week exclusive of any interests on investment: There are no county almshouses in Massachusetts, as poor relief matters are handled by the city and town governments. The number of almshouses in the state is about 140, which is considerably less than the number fifteen years ago. With/ the exception of one almshouse which is maintained jointly by eighteen towns, there are no union almshouses in Massachusetts although it is a common practice for one almshouse to take as boarders paupers in need of institutional care from neighboring cities and towns having no almshouses of their own.

. Certain cities, some having a population as large as 40,000, have no almshouses; and more than half of the towns have no almshouses, these communities depend almost entirely upon outdoor relief to take care of those in need of aid.

Very few married couples are sent to the almshouse, probably not over fifteen married couples being almshouse inmates at the present time. Ordinarily married couples in our almshouses are permitted to occupy the same quarters.

OLD AGE PENSIONS IN OHIO.

THOMAS J. DONNELLY

Secretary, Ohio Federation of Labor and Member, Ohio Commission on Health Insurance and Old Age Pensions

The subject of Old Age Pensions is receiving a good deal of attention in some of the other States of the Union besides Pennsylvania, and it is for this reason that I am here today from Ohio as a representative of labor.

As perhaps many of you know, Ohio began the study of this question in 1917, following the action of the Ohio Legislature on a bill providing for the appointment of a commission to study the subject of sickness and "to make inquiry into the subject of old age in its relation to industry and to the public interest and of the adequacy of existing methods of caring for aged workers." The commission made an exhaustive study of the subject, making a report to the Governor of Ohio and the 1919 General Assembly. As a result of the recommendations of the commission, bills were introduced in the General Assembly to promote the public health and to provide State Old Age Pensions. The public health bill met with little opposition and became a law. Not so with the Old Age Pension bill. No action could be obtained by the Legislature thereon.

The Ohio State Federation of Labor then took up the campaign for Old Age Pensions and had introduced in the General Assembly of 1921 the bill for Old Age Pensions which had been before the General Assembly in 1919. This effort to secure the passage of Old Age Pension legislation was also unsuccessful. The State Federation of Labor then decided to initiate a bill on this subject. This was done in 1922, in cooperation with the Fraternal Order of Eagles. The Legislature again failed to act, and supplementary initiative petitions were then circulated to bring the bill to a direct vote of the people. The required number of signatures to the supplementary petitions were secured and the measure went on the ballot in November 1923. Unfortunately, this occurred at a time when the people of Ohio were in revolt against two taxation measure passed by the 1923 Legislature, and which measures had been car ried to the electorate through the operation of the referendom. I addition to this, the advocates of Old Age Pensions were confrontee by the same campaign of misrepresentation by its opponents and th magnifying of costs of Old Age Pensions as they have met, as understand it, in Pennsylvania. The measure was defeated at th polls, along with the obnoxious tax measures, though the bill re ceived approximately 400,000 votes.

The campaign for Old Age Pensions has not ended in Ohio, bui rather, has just commenced. Supporters of Old Age Pensions i: Ohio realize, however, that it will require the furnishing of muc] data to the citizenship on the subject and the conducting of a: educational campaign before it can be hoped to enact legislatio: on the subject in Ohio. We are confident that once the electorat receives accurate information on the subject and comes to realiz the need of such legislation, it will be enacted. This campaign o education in Ohio and elsewhere appears to me to be the work o the hour for the advocates of Old Age Pensions. I am confiden that once our facts and arguments are carried to the electorate, fairly accurate estimate of the costs given, and all of the beneficia effects of the proposed legislation made clear, that Old Age Pensio: legislation will follow quickly. When that time comes, many o those now opposed to the proposition because of lack of informatio in relation thereto will wonder why they had previously opposed ii

Aside from the necessity for such legislation at the present tim as a social measure, Labor is advocating it because of the revolutio caused by machinery in production, which, through intensive laboi shortens the earning period of the wage earner in many industria enterprises, thereby eliminating him from industry at an age whe: he should be employed and engaged in striving to provide a con petency for his old age. These conditions are producing unemploy ment among numbers of vigorous and skilled citizens, and is pre senting the problem of old age dependency. Society must face th problem of industry and age, and solve it, or provide pensions fo those thus displaced and becoming dependent in their old age.

Pennsylvania has taken the lead in this matter for the industria States, and I sincerely trust that a way may be found to overcon the decision by one of your courts declaring your legislation u: constitutional, and that your Old Age Assistance Commission ma be permitted to continue to pioneer in this field of Old Age Pension

THE POOR HOUSE IN ILLINOIS.

WILLIAM MITCHELL

Member, Old Age Pension Committee, United Mine Workers of America

The Old Age Pension Committee of the United Mine Workei of America has been conducting an investigation of the cost an conditions of caring for unfortunate dependents in the state c Illinois under the Poorhouse System. This Committee has paid

Personal visit to eighty of the county homes of the state. We have found conditions varying from the very best to the most horrible, largely dependent upon the whims and capability of County Supervisors and Superintendents.

The eighty homes visited comprise 14,417 acres of land, valued at $2,565,425.00 with buildings and furnishing valued at $6,176,279.00, making a total investment of $8,741,704.00. In these institutions there are at the present time 2,684 inmates. Allowing four per cent on the investment would mean $130.00 to each inmate. Add to this the average cost of maintainence which is, according to the figures furnished us, $5.30 per week, or $275.60 per annum, making a total cost of $405.60 per annum. In addition to this sum something should be allowed for insurance and repairs so that we find the present system to be a costly one to say nothing of the cruel and inhuman method employed in caring for our aged and helpless dependents.

Of the 2,684 inmates, 2,177 are 65 years of age and over; of these 870 could readily find good homes if paid a reasonable pension not to exceed $300.00 per annum, according to the statements of the various Superintendents, and a much larger per cent, according to interviews held with the inmates. We also found that the combined salary of the Superintendents of these institutions amount to $104,778.00 annually; attending physicians $27,607.00 in salaries, while quite a number are paid by the visit; and about $73,406.00 are paid for extra help. Of the eighty Superintendents interviewed, fifty-three favor old age pensions, eight are opposed and nineteen are doubtful. The Superintendents in addition to their salaries are furnished with a residence and living expenses.

Even in the very best of the county institutions, those where the inmates had nothing but praise for their treatment, it was a touching sight to see how their old faces would light up with joy and hope at the mere suggestion of a pension that would enable them to go home, however humble it might be, and live and die among friends, familiar scenes and happy associations now lost to them forever.

CHAPTER X.

DO PENNSYLVANIA EMPLOYERS FAVOR STATE OLD AGE ASSISTANCE?

In view of the fact that the proceedings questioning the constitutionality of the Pennsylvania Old Age Assistance Act have been instituted by a number of large employers of labor, many have wondered whether a considerable part of this antagonism was not the result of a lack of understanding, on the part of these employers, of the provisions of the Old Age Assistance Law. For, inasmuch as industry is largely responsible and faced with the problem of the superannuated employee; and, the further fact that increasingly industrial corporations are seeking to devise means of pensioning their old employees, it would seem that industrial leaders would be among the first to champion a state-wide old age assistance plan which would provide an adequate method of care of their superannuated workers.

During the discussions at the November Conference; Commission David S. Ludlum, who is himself a large employer of labor, express(it as his opinion that the law when fully in operation would enab employers not only to give employment but also to continue in e ployment a very much larger percentage of the aged than is the ca today. It was his opinion that many an aged person would not on be too glad to continue his work but that some work could found for him even in modern industry were it not for the fa that employers, who very frequently are handling corporate stockholders money, feel loath to add to the organization men a women of advanced ages for fear that they would have a mor obligation to continue to give these men some support althoug they may become too old to perform their duties. If the employ knew that the aged workers would be able to receive some a sistance under the present law, the experiences of the older worke could be utilized to a greater extent.

In order to ascertain the trend of opinion among employers labor in regard to Commissioner Ludlum's view, a letter, requesti their opinions on Mr. Ludlum's suggestions, was sent to about or hundred employers in the State selected at random from a li in the application files of the Commission. A similar letter w addressed to the members of our county boards whose experien with applicants would enable them to present some definite vie on the matter. A few of the statements so far received are present herewith:

"I believe the position taken by Mr. David S. Ludlum to the fect that were such an old age assistance act put into effect, t tendency would be to employ older men to some considerable exte is based on good ground. I know that in our own case, we wo gladly employ older men were it not for such conditions.

The East Broad Top Railroad Co."

"I believe the idea expressed above is correct. At this plant try to take care of our older employees, but there is always so hesitation about placing an elderly man on the pay roll.

Armstrong Cork Company."

"We are not familiar with the Act for Old Age Assistance, b if it will assist worthy old people we feel that it is a Godly Act.

"We agree with Mr. Ludlum that aged persons who are able to wo would only be too glad to continue at their work if allowed to do We also believe that any employer would hire a young or mid aged man in preference to an elderly man.

The Pittsburgh & Lake Erie Railroad Co.'

"The writer is in hearty accord with any movement along this li In the manufacturing plant we find it a burden to carry a of old men that we are unable to shift around to the most effici position during this protracted slack period—if we lay them off suspend them it looks to them like plain and deliberate discrimi tion to evade a pension (although there is not one such instance) a causes dissatisfaction among all our employees.

"It would seem to the writer that some system governed thro some central or State agency applying to all employees in all dustries within the State is the only satisfactory soluion of t

· If some. such arrangement could be. made and sup-
l the people within the State it would be about one-
oposition it now appears to be for the reason that it
p now unknown avenues of employment in all indus-
older and now undesirable employees.
sion would state that the writer earnestly hopes that
ot far distant when the manufacturers at large will
estion from the right angle and get together along
ctive line."

Nationl Transit Pump & Machine Co."

o Commissioner David S. Ludlum's suggestion, we be-
s a good thing and can heartily recommend the same.

Penn Bridge Company."

·ell aware of the many problems which present them-
nection with employment of the aged. We, ourselves,
ongly that it is the duty of the employer to take care
n who have given long and faithful service during
of life when· they are partly or totally incapicitated,
, from fulfilling their former duties. We look with
any action which will tend to alleviate the hardships
he present time and we shall be very glad to give our
any movement of this kind if it is practical and
nable limits.

Textile Machine Works."

I believe, when same becomes operative, is one that will
commendation of all employers. Personally, I am
avor of same.

Alumina Shale Brick Company."

· are not informed very fully about this law, we think
ld be very much in favor of same.

Hocking Coal Company."

·ely agree with the opinion of Mr. Ludlum as to the
provision of this kind upon the employees that are
years.
along with other manufacturing concerns, been com-
ce the view that employees get old soon enough under
ment without hiring elderly men that are likely to become
on someone, and the company whom they have served
feel obligated to some extent in taking care of them.
ge Assistance would make it very much easier to take
is kind when we feel that some provision has been made
ter they are no longer able to work. We, therefore,

"We are not thoroughly familiar with this Act but are in sympathy with any movement that will benefit aged persons who are worthy of such help.

.Culler Furniture Company."

"I know taking care of aged employees in industry is quite a problem today and the question confronts us quite often.

American Chain Company, Inc."

"We have not the heart to dismiss an old employee on account of age. This we guard against by not taking on any more very old men. It is easier to refuse employment, than it is to let one go.
In our opinion no manufacturing plant can afford to be a charitable institution, except only in a few rare cases.

Lewisburg Mills."

"Many of our workmen are 'old men' as the world today would class them and we do not think our stockholders are seriously objecting.

Samuel J. Shimer & Sons."

"The policy of this Company has always been to aid its old employees. We usually find some light task around our plants for such employees, and we have also covered all our employees with what we call Group Insurance. We firmly believe when an employee had given long and faithful service, he is entitled to some consideration, and we have under advisement at the present time a plan to make this proposition more effective.

Union Drawn Steel Company."

"The writer's opinion coincides with that of Mr. David S. Ludlum. Our policy is to take care of employees regardless of their ability to work if any disability is caused by old age, and this very feature governs our employment department in taking into consideration the age of new men. If the employer understood that the aged workers were entitled to receive some outside assistance there would, without doubt, be a greater utilization of their efforts. Without doubt, this would be a benefit both to employer and employee.

Montgomery Table & Desk Works."

"I think the Old Age Assistance Act is all right.

Mussina Heiser & Company."

"We think Commissioner Ludlum's opinion is right.

Bowman Fuel Company."

"We concur in opinion of Mr. Ludlum.

Eagle Iron Company."

"I am of the same opinion as Mr. Ludlum, that a great deal of the opposition to this Act can be eliminated by a thorough understanding of the same.

O. W. Supply Company."

"I agree with the above.

H. C. Frick Coke Company—Scottdale Plant."

"I am inclined to agree with Commissioner David S. Ludlum. I believe that the installing of an old age assistance would of itself prompt employers to keep employees who have reached a fairly good age, and also to employ them. That would be preferable to supporting them idly. It is within my knowledge that some concerns have fixed an age limit of forty-five years.

Beaver Valley Traction Company."

"We are heartily in accord with Mr. Ludlum's ideas concerning this act. We happen to have in our employ men well up into the 70's who are quite efficient; however, we have men in their 60's who are not as efficient, in fact, some of them have outlived their usefulness in industry.

Penn Central Light & Power Company."

Opinions somewhat differing from those of Commissioner Ludlum are contained in the following comments which represent all we received:

"I feel that the opinion of Commissioner David S. Ludlum, President of the Autocar Company, is a very good one. I do, however, feel that the aged are pretty well taken care of in the State at the present time; I know they are in our own county.

. If there is any need for Old Age Pensions, I do not believe that this should be saddled on to the State as an extra expense, but that it should be taken care of by contributions to insurance funds by the workmen themselves. I think that the principle of gratuities without sacrifice on the part of the beneficiary is entirely opposed to the economic welfare of our people.

Stackpole Carbon Company."

"We are of the opinion that the real desirable workman does not desire charity, but prepares for old age by laying by a part of his earnings to carry him through old age, as an independent citizen. A system of bonuses paid to employees for efficiency, by all corporations, would in my opinion be a more satisfactory solution than pensions by the Commonwealth.

American Window Glass Company."

"We are sorry we cannot agree with the tone of your letter as to Mr. Ludlum's opinion of the benefits of the Old Age Assistance Act in order to keep men in industry longer.

"We are very much afraid that sooner or later, in fact as it became generally known, it would be used as a regular excuse in industry to cut an old man's wage and tell him to apply to the Old Age Commission for the balance of it. This may seem to be a pretty harsh statement to make, but we feel perfectly confident that it is just what would happen, not with everybody, of course, but with too many entirely and that you are killing just what we imagine you are trying to undertake.

"Our idea of an old age assistance would be to keep the old man out of the poorhouse and the State only contribute to him such an amount as it would figure it would cost the State or County to support him in the poorhouse. If an old man can be supported by the State or County outside of the poorhouse for the same amount, we consider it desirable.

Sheppard & Myers, Inc."

The following are some of the comments made by members
County Old Age Assistance Boards:

"In making a survey of the County for the Old Age Assista
Board, I came in contact with a great many men who hired a
found employment for men. Their greatest objection in employ
men over sixty years old was that if they were able to do the w
until they were seventy, they would have a moral obligation to g
these men some help, which they could not afford. Some men told
that often they would be hurt, have an accident, and the comp
would feel they would be responsible, but if they knew there would
some help for them when they could no longer hold the position tl
now hold they would be given employment for several years long
I have several applications for old age assistance to whom the c
pany for whom they have worked for years are paying their bo
to keep them from the County Home. They are very anxiously w
ing for an old age assistance.

Beaver County Old Age Assistance Board.

"From what experience I have had on this Board in Crawf
County, I will say that I believe Mr. Ludlum's opinion is all corr
and that if some of those who are opposing this very worthy ass
ance could only be with some of the investigators and see the desti
tion that is prevalent in some places where we have been, they wou
no doubt, take a different stand on this very worthy cause.

Crawford County Old Age Assistance Board.

"We fully agree with Mr. Ludlum's opinion. One of the employ
at the Bessemer here recently made the same statement.

Mercer County Old Age Assistance Board.

"I fully believe that 75 per cent of the present old people emplo
by corporations would be maintained a much longer period if
Old Age Assistance was properly functioning; and also 25 per
that are not now employed would find employment if same wer
force.

Tioga County Old Age Assistance Board

"I agree with Mr. Ludlum in regard to the employment of the a
I went to the office of the Herksion & Walker Brick Company of
Union in regard to an applicant and they seemed very willing to l
an aged man in their employ providing he would get a little assist
later on. I think quite a few firms turn people out when they bec
old thinking they might have them to keep when they are unabl
work.

Huntingdon County Old Age Assistance Board

"From an acquaintance during more than forty years of busi
association I may say that with the Old Age Assistance Ac
operation it will materially benefit a class of our citizens, both
and women, who require assistance at this period of life.

"Some of them might secure an opportunity to labor at some k
of work were it not for the fact of the railroads' age limit in hi
employees; and this applies to our powder plants and other in
tries employing labor here.

"It would seem that this Old Age Assistance Act in opera
would benefit some of our most worthy citizens and not be detri
tal to any of our people.

Cameron County Old Age Assistance Boarc

"I heartily endorse Commissioner Ludlum's idea in regard to employers retaining employees of advanced age while capable of performing anything near their ordinary earning capacity.

"For thirty-five years, I have been employing men of practically all ages, and my experience has been that men of mature years are more trustworthy . . . and in most instances more efficient than young men."

Bedford County Old Age Assistance Board."

"I quite agree with Commissioner Ludlum that a very considerable portion of the opposition to the Old Age Act is due to the lack of a full appreciation of its provisions. The law when in operation would certainly enable employers to give employment to a very much larger percentage of the aged if the employer knew the aged would not become an obligation to them when they became too old to perform their duties.

"It is quite pathetic the way the old people of our County came forth to file their application blanks and I can assure you it will be a pleasure to the County Board if the time comes for us to tell them that the Law is in effect.

Venango County Old Age Assistance Board."

"It seems to me that if an old age assistance fund were available, it would be a help in keeping a number of old men employed in our industries. It would stimulate heads of corporations to retain men who are up in years, knowing that in so doing they would not be liable for their keep in future years. Nine out of every ten people to whom I talked to relative to the Commission are in favor of it.

Clarion County Old Age Assistance Board."

"I fully agree with the opinion of Mr. David S. Ludlum relative to employers carrying on their payrolls men and women of advanced years; it would be fine if the 'old age assistance' idea could be carried out.

Warren County Old Age Assistance Board."

"Undoubtedly much of the opposition to the Old Age Assistance Act is due to the lack of a full appreciation of its provisions.

"I feel quite sure from conversations with employers that many would give employment to the aged if they felt no moral obligation to give these men and women support when they become too old to work; and if all employers knew the aged worker would be able to receive some assistance under the law, aged workers would be given employment.

Berks County Old Age Assistance Board."

"It is a very sad state of affairs when our Board receives such a large number of applications and letters appealing to the assistance board for help.

"I heartily endorse the opinion and expression of Mr. David S. Ludlum and I trust there will be no let up until the assistance of aged and dependent becomes an effective law.

Susquehanna County Old Age Assistance Board."

"Mr. Ludlum's view in the matter of aged persons getting more employment under the Old Age Assistance Act when put in operation is in my opinion a very correct one. I know Civil War veterans who

did more work, and worked harder after receiving aid from t
Government than they did before. That it would be an induceme
for others to employ them is, beyond a doubt, true of the Old A
Assistance Act. It also would be an incentive for them to he
themselves outside of what they might receive from the Act.

Fulton County Old Age Assistance Board."

"After reading Mr. David S. Ludlum's expression, and from 1
experience as Secretary of Mifflin County Old Age Assistance Boa1
I heartily approve the the same. If the employer knew that t
aged workers would be able to receive some assistance under t
present law, older workers would be utilized to a much greater exte:

Mifflin County Old Age Assistance Board."

"I have talked to lawyers, doctors, coal operators (the farme
especially) and all favor it. I really believe there is no oppositi
to the Act in Somerset County.

"If one meets forty to fifty of these dependents and their supporte
and they explain to you the conditions as they really are, you canr
help but feel as David S. Ludlum, President of the Autocar Compai
when he expressed the belief that a very considerable portion of t
opposition to this Act is due to the lack of a full appreciation of :
provisions.

Somerset County Old Age Assistance Board."

"I am thoroughly in accord with Mr. Ludlum's views. I feel it
our duty, as a Christian Civilized Community to assist the aged.

Clinton County Old Age Assistance Board."

"From my own experience I find that the applicants for Old A
Assistance that I have investigated would not be able to work at ε
they are too old and feeble for even light manual labor. We ha
only investigated a portion of the applications in this County, k
so far as we have gone I think my statement is correct.

Westmoreland County Old Age Assistance Board."

"Concerning Mr. Ludlum's expression I would say he has express
what a great majority of people are thinking. As he states, the
are a number who might continue working at some light work
they were assured some slight financial aid when they are pε
working.

Sullivan County Old Age Assistance Board."

"I do not hold the same opinion that Mr. Ludlum holds. Pract
ally all the applications that our Board passed upon are persc
who are not able to work even if they had a chance.. His opini
may hold good in other counties but not in ours.

Adams County Old Age Assistance Board."

"Mr. Ludlum's opinion is based upon large experience and gen
ous sympathies. Other employers of different temperament mig
readily find grounds to oppose his kindliness. To some the o1
consideration is the size of the product which can be squeezed c
of the employees.

Monroe County Old Age Assistance Board."

"I considered Mr. Ludlum's address one of the best given. In our city or county when a man or woman reaches the age of 60 and 65 they are considered too old to be given employment to and they are advised that work is slack and the plant will close down for a short time; that is one way of getting rid of old material. When work is resumed, the old employees are forgotten and younger men are employed. I have worked weekly in our County Home for a period of twenty-five years and I know a number of our old people would not be in our home if they could find some employment and be given some assistance. It is very difficult when you have been active all your life and then have to come down and sit on a bench or working chair without anything to occupy your time or mind.

York County Old Age Assistance Board."

"I have no way of knowing just how different organizations look upon the subject but from the expression of the people, there is no doubt that the public heartily approves of the Act. From personal investigation and review of applications I believe that ninety per cent of the applicants are worthy of assistance and county aid alone is not sufficient.

"Mr. David S. Ludlum certainly makes a good argument from the point of view of the employer.

McKean County Old Age Assistance Board.'

"Mr. Ludlum struck the nail on the head when he vouched this opinion; there is no doubt that this is very largely the case with the greater percentage of employers of labor and, if employers had the assurance that their aged workers would receive some assistance under such a law as the Old Age Assistance Act, they would find some employment of a light nature for many whom they dismiss at ages ranging from 45 years to 60 years. As it now is, what savings such aged have when their employments are terminated, it is all used up by the time they reach the age of 70 years and, at that age, most of them become dependent on the assistance of others.

"Practically all applicants in this county for assistance under the Old Age Assistance Act, stated they would prefer to do some light work at a wage sufficient to 'just live' rather than apply for the assistance afforded by the Act, but that employers tell them they are too old and will not employ them.

Lycoming County Old Age Assistance Board."

OPINIONS FROM ABROAD

January 15, 1925.

The following recent letters are significant:

"I have no hesitation in saying—and I am sure that everybody in this country would agree with me—that the Old Age Pensions Act is the most popular piece of social legislation ever passed in this country. There is not a vestige of opposition to it, and nobody would ever dream of suggesting its repeal. On the contrary, there is a strong agitation among all political parties for its improvement. The question of Old Age Pensions is a non-party issue in Great Britain. It is heartily supported by all parties."

Philip Snowden,
Former Chancellor of the Exchequer,
Great Britian
February 18, 1925.

"The experience of the Pensions Administration is that the system has operated successfully. Our experience has been that the operation of the pensions law has in no way injured the morale of people because of its protection in old age, nor has it been found to discourage thrift. On the contrary, reviews of pensions have frequently shown that, after being granted pensions the recipients have commenced to earn, or, if already in employment, that they have considerably increased their earnings and in various ways added to their property."

J. R. Collins,
Commissioner of Pensions,
Australia

STATEMENT OF EXPENDITURES OF OLD AGE ASSISTANCE COMMISSION FROM SEPTEMBER 6, 1923 to NOVEMBER 30, 1924.

Salaries of Staff	$7,128.29
Fees of Commision	270.00
Traveling Expenses	1,800.85
Telegraph and Telephone	179.48
Postage	331.00
Office Equipment	279.06
Office Supplies	371.27
Printing	108.57
Miscellaneous	142.97
Total	$10,611.49

APPENDIX I

NAMES AND ADDRESSES OF MEMBERS OF COUNTY OLD AGE ASSISTANCE BOARD.

ADAMS
Hiram C. Lady, Chairman......................Arendtsville
Mrs. Wm. Arch, McClean, ...Gettysburg
Hugh E. Topper.............................McSherrystown
C. E. Tawney, Secretary........................Gettysburg

BEAVER
Mrs. W. B. Gray, Secretary....................Beaver Falls
(Two vacancies)

BEDFORD
B. C. May, Chairman..........................Hyndman
H. G. Smith, Secretary........................Bedford
W. J. Van Horn...............................Everett

BERKS
J. H. Reichert, Chairman......................Reading
Mrs. Herbert J. Vastine, Secretary............Reading
Seibert L. Witman............................Reading

BRADFORD
David J. Armstrong...........................Monroeton
John C. Mather...............................Ulster
Mrs. Josephine Waldo, Secretary.................Wyalusing

BUTLER
D. G. Bastain, Chairman......................Zelienople
Mrs. R. C. Wiggins, Secretary.................Butler
T. P. Mifflin...............................North Washington

CAMBRIA
Mrs. Lester Larimer, Chairman ....Patton
Mrs. A. M. Stineman, Secretary.................South Fork
Miss Loretto Prindible........................Patton

CAMERON
J. P. McNarney, Chairman......................Emporium
Mrs. Hattie Smith, Secretary..................Driftwood
L. K. Huntington.............................Emporium

CENTRE
Mrs. Mazie Brouse, Chairman...................Bellefonte
Mrs. Rebecca Tuten, Secretary.................Philipsburg
Mrs. Annie Fisher...........................Centre Hall

CHESTER
Amos G. Gotwals, Chairman....................Phoenixville
Mrs. L. F. Lambert, Secretary.................Coatesville, R. D.
J. D. Moore................................Oxford

CLARION
    H. H. Bittenbender......................... Shippenville
    James Pinks............................... Clarion
    J. W. F. Wilkinson......................... Clarion

CLEARFIELD
    George M. Rosser, Chairman................. Clearfield
    Howard Stewart, Secretary.................. Clearfield
    James W. Ruffner........................... Madera

CLINTON
    Mrs. Helen M. Mayes, Secretary............. Lock Haven
    Mrs. Chas. Osner........................... Renovo
    (One vacancy)

COLUMBIA
    A. N. Shearer, Chairman.................... Berwick
    R. W. Young, Secretary..................... Catawissa
    H. A. Kemp................................. Bloomsburg

CRAWFORD
    M. G. Beatty, Chairman..................... Meadville
    Howard Powell, Secretary.................. Cochranton
    N. W. Reynolds............................. Titusville

ERIE
    A. J. McCollum, Chairman................... Erie
    N. W. Couse, Secretary..................... North East
    C. C. Rice................................. Union City

FAYETTE
    R. S. McCrum............................... Uniontown
    (Two vacancies)

FULTON
    Luther Kirk, Chairman...................... Hustontown
    Ulysses Humbert, Secretary................. Big Cove Tannery
    Ross R. Hann............................... Harrisonville

GREENE
    W. R. Hogue, Chairman...................... Waynesburg
    Miss Mary W. Denny, Secretary.............. Waynesburg
    E. S. Minor................................ Jefferson

HUNTINGDON
    George W. Fisher, Chairman................. Warriorsmark
    Mrs. Mamie Harper Swan, Secretary.......... Shade Gap
    Allison Black.............................. Broad Top City

INDIANA
    Alex M. Stewart, Chairman.................. Indiana
    Mrs. Carrie H. Stitt, Secretary............ Blairsville
    Dr. William A. Simpton..................... Indiana

JEFFERSON
    Russell Sheldon, Chairman.................. Punxsutawney
    Mrs. Geo. W. Means, Secretary.............. Brooksville
    C. R. Hall................................. Reynoldsville

LACKAWANNA
George G. Brooks, Chairman..................... Scranton
Mrs. Margaret G. Jadwin, Secretary.............. Scranton
P. F. Calpin................................... Scranton

LAWRENCE
Robert K. Aiken, Chairman..................... New Castle
Mrs. Nettie G. Matheny, Secretary.............. New Castle
Rev. Charles Bell............................. Ellwood City

LYCOMING
James F. Collier, Chairman..:................... Williamsport
D. W. Osler................................... Hughesville
Shem Spigelmyer............................... Jersey Shore
John A. Harries, Secretary..................... Williamsport

McKEAN
Miss Mae Choate, Chairman..................... Smethport
Miss Margaret Caldwell, Secretary.............. Bradford
Mrs. Fantine Burdick.......................... Kane

MERCER
Mrs. H. K. Daughtery, Chairman................. Grove City
Mrs. Stacy Dean, Secretary..................... Greenville
Mrs. John C. Owsley...:........................ Sharon

MIFFLIN
Frank E. Mann, Chairman....................... Lewistown
J. Harry Sides, Secretary...................... McVeytown
Miss Elizabeth H. Garver....:.................. Belleville

MONROE
Luther Hoffman, Chairman...................... East Stroudsburg
Dr. W. R. Fisher, Secretary.................... Swiftwater
Dr. Mary Erdman............................... Stroudsburg

MONTOUR
Geo. B. Kase, Chairman........................ Danville
Mrs. Sara B. Jennings, Secretary............... Danville
Levi Fenstermacher............................ Danville

NORTHUMBERLAND
Hon. John M. Mack, Chairman................... Shamokin
Harry Strine, Secretary..:..................... Milton
Dr. C. M. Gass................................ Sunbury

PERRY
Hon. C. M. Bower, Chairman.................... Blain
G. H. Frank, Secretary........................ Newport
G. W. Meck.................................... New Bloomfield

PIKE
John C. Warner, Chairman..:................... Milford
John E. Almer, Secretary...................... Milford
Miss Ethel Noyes..:........................... Milford

POTTER
A. F. Smith, Chairman.........................Coudersport
Mrs. W. W. Thompson, Secretary................Coudersport
Mrs. W. F. Dubois............................Coudersport

SNYDER
M. W. S. Benfer..............................Beaver Springs
Banks Kreamer................................Richfield
David Woomer................................Mt Pleasant Mills

SOMERSET
W. L. Mills, Chairman........................Markleton
Howard B. Forney, Secretary..................Davidsville
J. M. Gnagey.................................Mydersdale

SULLIVAN
Mrs. Orrill Avery, Secretary.................Forkesville
W. B. Snyder.................................Nordmont
Mrs. Elizabeth Walsh.........................Dushore

SUSQUEHANNA
Joseph West, Chairman........................Fairdale
F. A. Osborn, Secretary......................Harford
Mrs. Katherine Irving........................Susquehanna

TIOGA
William Ordway, Chairman.....................Elkland
Leon Baynes, Secretary.......................Mansfield
James L. Lattimer............................Sabinsville

UNION
Dr. John T. Judd, Chairman...................Lewisburg
Rev. R. Ira Gass, Secretary..................West Milton
H. B. Young..................................Mifflinburg

VENANGO
Mrs. E. E. Pundt, Chairman...................Oil City
Mrs. Core M. Dille, Secretary................Cooperstown
Mrs. A. B. Corrin............................Franklin

WARREN
E. M. Hodges, Chairman.......................Warren
Mrs. Robert Hall, Secretary..................Warren
Dr. L. E. Chapman............................Warren

WASHINGTON
Mr. T. F. Burte..............................Washington
Dr. J. K. Smith..............................Charleroi
Mrs. Janet Workman, Secretary................Canonsburg

WESTMORELAND
Frank D. Neale, Chairman.....................Vandergrift
Mrs. John C. Silsley, Secretary..............Greensburg
Joseph E. Stevenson..........................West Newton

YORK
Frederick Z. Stauffer, Chairman..............York
Edwin S. Crone, Secretary....................York
Mrs. Susan H. Frank..........................York